I was standing close to the doors when a Vietnamese man loosely swathed in body bandages swept through on his stretcher. His left arm dangled oddly out of the wrappings and brushed against me as he went past. The arm fell off, thumping onto the floor. Someone retrieved it immediately, but I found myself gaping and gasping in shock. More wounded poured in—men waving bloody stumps, men without feet, men with steaming holes in their torsos, men whose heads were missing clumps of hair and skull.

The floor got slimy, then became awash in gore. Human parts and bright crimson bandages and fluids sluiced together, welling up until I could no longer see the bottoms of my boots. Men screamed and begged for their mothers without restraint or embarrassment. It was the most monstrously sickening scene I had ever beheld or ever would.

# NOT BY THE BOOK

## A Combat Intelligence Officer in Vietnam

## Eric Smith

IVY BOOKS • NEW YORK

Ivy Books
Published by Ballantine Books
Copyright © 1993 by Eric Smith

Library of Congress Catalog Card Number: 93-91592

ISBN 0-8041-0796-3

Manufactured in the United States of America

First Edition: December 1993

To JanElaine, who told me so, again.

# ACKNOWLEDGMENTS

Chris Beard, Bill Brill, Brian Daley, Cheryl Doyle, Hugh Eckert, Tommy Flaherty, Mark Gatlin, Joe Gross, Owen Lock, Gerard Smith, Lucia St. Clair Robson, Helen Spinelli, and Wick Tourison—you all know what you did and why I am grateful to you.

Special thanks to Otto the Rumpled Writer.

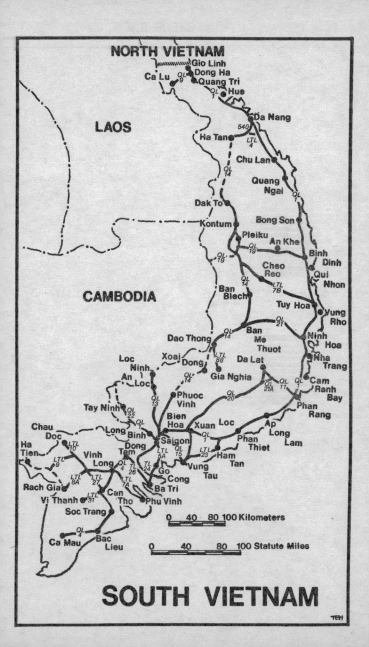

# Introduction

I'm aware of all those army intelligence jokes. Don't think I'm not.

"Army intelligence is a contradiction in terms."

"Military intelligence is to intelligence what military music is to music."

Ha, ha.

Many of these cruel quips have arisen since we fought in Vietnam, and I can see why. In retrospect it looks like intelligence work by all U.S. armed forces was less than spectacularly successful—or at least it was *perceived* that way.

I'm not sure I agree with the critics, the nonmilitary ones especially. Nor can I claim that the intelligence services should have been awarded shiny medals of merit, either.

The truth is that I saw our intelligence effort in Vietnam from the very bottom—first at the division level, then at an infantry brigade—and I am thus poorly qualified to judge the overall success or failure of it.

I will say this, however; the *system*, at least, was well designed. The way we gathered information and evaluated it was as effective as any that could be devised for use in a far-off country with a vastly different culture and a fanatically motivated enemy. In theory, anyway.

It was only in the execution of the plan that things tended to fall apart, particularly at the combat intelligence level where I was. Information we collected was often tainted, inaccurate, unchecked, or unverifiable. Then it went to the next higher headquarters, where all of its shortcomings were incorporated into even larger compilations of doubtful information from other sources. And so on.

Maybe the weaknesses of the U.S. Army intelligence effort reflected the weaknesses of the U.S. Army in Vietnam at large: we had the best intentions and the worst luck.

And speaking of luck, mine was pretty putrid. I entered active duty in 1967 when the war in Vietnam had already arrived at the dead serious stage. After a year of training, some of it relevant, some of it absurdly useless, I was flown to Vietnam for the standard one-year tour in 1968. I left with all fingers and toes (but not emotions) intact in the spring of 1969.

Now it turns out that, from a strictly statistical point of view, the period 1968–69 was about the nastiest one in the history of American involvement in that corner of Southeast Asia.

I have seen published numbers indicating that if you were a first lieutenant stationed in I Corps (northern South Vietnam) in 1968–69, your chances of being wounded or killed were better than almost anyone's. Of course these statistics applied mainly to infantrymen, but as a former first lieutenant who served in I Corps in 1968–69, I feel justified in breathing a belated sigh of relief. Or even retroactively hyperventilating a little bit.

But now, more than twenty years after I landed at Fort Lewis, Washington, and gratefully kissed the good ground of home, it's time for a reassessment of the period I spent as a staff intelligence officer with the American Division in Chu Lai in the presently defunct Republic of South Vietnam.

I say *re*assessment because my first personal assessments, made over the several years after I came home, were negative and biased and colored by the negative, biased attitude of the nation to which I returned. Today I am a lot older and a little bit smarter. I should have some perspective by now.

Still, I experienced Vietnam as a junior intelligence officer, and I may yet slip back into a junior officer's attitude as I talk about the pros and cons of the methods we employed there.

Forgive me if I do. I am middle-aged only by virtue of

the years I've been alive. When it comes to reliving my spell in Vietnam, it is all too easy to become twenty-three years old again.

In the narrative that follows, I have frequently changed names to protect the innocent . . . and the guilty.

# CHAPTER 1

# School Days

I graduated from Georgetown University in Washington, D.C. In the early 1960s it was known as a second-rate Harvard for rich Catholic kids who liked to party. It was also known for its School of Foreign Service, which brought students from all over the world to play at embassy parties and learn how to be minor consulate officials.

Buried under all the froufrou of Georgetown's lightweight reputation, however, was a no-frills college of liberal arts that insisted on the basics and taught them well. Georgetown was a conservative institution at heart, and as proof of that, it maintained a robust ROTC (Reserve Officer Training Corps) program for the Army and the Air Force.

I joined the Army ROTC in my freshman year for two reasons: (1) I had a natural, longstanding interest in military matters; (2) My mother demanded that I join so I wouldn't end up as a buck private draftee someday.

During my four years in cadet uniform (once a week, on Tuesdays), I was given minimum exposure to the tenets of the intelligence game. We concentrated more on infantry tactics and mindless drill on the athletic field. It slowly dawned on me over the years, however, that Georgetown contributed far more than its normal share of officer graduates to the branch of the U.S. Army known as military intelligence.

To this day, I still don't know why. I can guess that it might have been due to the intellectual caliber of the students, the college's location in the nation's capital, or the foreign service program offered at Georgetown. There's no

4

way to tell for sure. After I went on active duty, I found that other universities around the country contributed disproportionate shares of graduates to certain branches of the army, too. The best and most ferocious infantry officers, for instance, always seemed to come from schools in Kentucky. Artillery officers hailed from Oklahoma more often than not, and so on. Who knows? Maybe the army maintained an unofficial quota system for its various branches based on some secret, arcane method of calculating which college was most likely to produce officers with certain characteristics.

In any case, I applied for military intelligence in my senior year, along with many of my classmates. My second and third choices were transportation corps and military police, respectively—neither of which excited me the way the sound of "military intelligence" did. The fact was, of course, that I knew practically nothing about the branch or its operations. It just sounded romantic.

Well, there was one *other* reason I applied. I was going to get both my college diploma and my commission as a second lieutenant in June of 1967. The Vietnam War was in full swing, and I knew my chances of being sent over were astronomically high. I figured, wrongly it turned out, that intelligence officers in Vietnam sat in air-conditioned Saigon villas, sipping iced tea and reading fascinating secret documents.

I wore glasses and had a nice liberal arts education from an eastern school. I didn't *do* combat. I assumed that the military intelligence branch would agree and assign me to an appropriately safe and intellectually stimulating post. At the very worst, I expected to be detailed to someplace civilized like West Germany, where I could sip cold beer, read fascinating secret documents, and pretend to be James Bond in uniform.

Besides, I hadn't done all that well in ROTC training. In weekend maneuvers during the school term and in one seven-week summer camp after junior year, I had displayed none of those natural infantry instincts that, say, the macho kids from Kentucky showed. Marching bored me, I avoided shining my boots, and I hated camping out. The strenuous life was not my bag, as we used to say in the sixties.

The U.S. Army, of course, could not have cared less about my fantasies and miscalculations. Sometime during my senior year (I don't remember exactly when), and after I had sent in my application to join the military intelligence branch (MI), I was tested along with other ROTC applicants for general intelligence skills.

(A note about army acronyms before we proceed. I will try to use military alphabet soup as sparingly as possible, but sometimes they're easier on your eyes and my typing fingers than the longer official name. MI is a good example. So bear with me as we go along.)

The tests, as I recall, were divided into two parts: image manipulation and language. The image section required the testee to mix and match sets of photographs, drawings, and complicated geometric figures. At the time, I had no idea what relevance any of this had to fighting godless Communism as an intelligence officer, but much later I figured out that people who did well in this test were eventually assigned to the image interpretation segment of MI. These fellows spent a lot of time inside darkened rooms, examining aerial photographs of enemy territory to find out what the enemy was up to.

The language part was easy for me. I was a constant reader and had already studied Latin (Catholic high-school requirement) and Spanish (in which I was quite fluent for an Irish kid from Brooklyn). I think I breezed through this part, which seemed to deal with general comprehension and manipulation of language rather than a specific tongue. I must have achieved a reasonably high score because I was accepted into MI and later assigned to Vietnamese language school.

The testing system seemed to be a bit limited, though. Surely MI officers did something besides stare at photos and talk to enemy prisoners. The MI branch contained area intelligence specialists, counterintelligence agents, electronic surveillance experts, administrators, and information-processing people of all kinds. Would image and language tests alone really sort out the different abilities of testees with varying backgrounds? Maybe MI only needed image interpreters and Vietnamese linguists that year?

I had one more obstacle to overcome before commissioning, however. Late in my final semester, I received a letter from MI branch headquarters summoning me to Fort McNair, a pleasant, slightly seedy, little administrative post located in downtown Washington. The letter said nothing about why I was being sent for, but it indicated as politely as possible that I should get my ass down to Fort McNair pronto.

I did.

When I arrived, I was shown to a small room furnished with only a table, two chairs, and a humming black box on the table. Wires fed out from the electrically noisy box to a set of wrist straps. To my inexperienced eyes it looked just like a lie detector. In a little while a sour-faced, middle-aged man in a rumpled suit walked in and, without preamble, demanded to know why I had lied on my application to the MI branch.

"I didn't lie at all," I replied. "What are you talking about?"

He must have been referring to the sheet of personal information I had filled out months before. It was one of what seemed like an interminable pile of questionnaires and forms I was asked to complete during the MI selection process.

"Listen, kid, you could be in big trouble here. This is a matter of national security. Now tell us the truth! Why did you lie on the background information form?"

"I'm sorry, sir, I must be stupid or something. I *told* the truth on all the forms MI gave me. Tell me what you're after, and I'll tell you whatever you want to know."

No answer. He then hooked me up to the black machine on the table, roughly strapping the leather cuffs on my wrists. He asked a few "establishing" questions, like my name, age, address, and school, and launched into a rapid-fire series of questions about my parents, my girlfriends, and finally my travel experiences.

My travel experiences? In the dim recesses of my mind, I began to get a faint idea of what he was searching for, but before I could say anything, my accuser walked out of the room, leaving me alone with the humming black box.

Five minutes or so later, another man opened the door and walked in. He was about the same age as the other one, but much more pleasant looking. His tie was loose, collar opened, sleeves up. He was smiling.

"Want a cigarette?" he asked. I took one, awkwardly because of the wrist cuffs. He lit it for me and one for himself.

"Mark is a little testy today," he said, obviously making reference to the obnoxious ogre I had been dealing with (and frightened by, frankly). "His wife's giving him a hard time, and I heard he had some health problems. Ulcer, I think."

As we puffed our cigarettes companionably, the new man said "So, what's the story about your trip to Europe?"

At this point I would have told him anything he wanted to know. How many times had I felt up my high-school girlfriend? Was I jealous of my father's attention to my little brother? Had I secretly lusted for the nun who taught me in first grade? Whatever. He was so much nicer and more civilized than the shithead who had strapped me to a machine and yelled at me that I was pathetically grateful to him. Suddenly, he seemed like a favorite uncle or a friendly big brother.

Later on, when I had finished my intelligence training and was in Vietnam, questioning terrified or hostile prisoners of war, I realized what had been going on that afternoon in Fort McNair. These guys, presumably civilian MI agents, were pulling the oldest trick in the spook book on me—the classic "white-hat–black-hat" routine, also known as "doing a Mutt and Jeff," after the famous cartoon characters.

It works quite simply. The first questioner is deliberately so nasty that the second questioner seems like a saint in comparison. The subject might resist the black hat, but the odds are that he or she will cave in gratefully to the white hat.

I, of course, fell for it totally. As soon as White Hat mentioned Europe, I blurted out "Oh, you mean Europe! You mean when I went to Europe with my family. On vacation! Right, I was there over a month, and . . ."

He stopped me with, "Why didn't you put all this on the background investigation form?"

Ransacking my mind for the right answer (it had to be right: this fine fellow was my bosom buddy, from whom I could not withhold the truth), I remembered that Sergeant Blineberry, the senior Georgetown ROTC noncom, had said that "no foreign travel earlier than five years ago needs to be mentioned" when he was instructing a group of us on how to fill out the form. Since I had gone on a trip to Spain, France, and Germany with my parents in the summer of 1962, I assumed that it would be irrelevant to mention it more than five years later in the winter of 1967.

Sergeant Blineberry was wrong, as he was on numerous other matters of army paperwork over the four years I knew him. "Chickenshit" was what he called anything that required him to put pen or pencil to paper, so it was no surprise to find out that Blineberry had misinformed me again on an item of hated paperwork.

In any case, I was more than glad to dump my guts to White Hat to clear up the whole problem. I explained Blineberry's role in making me omit Europe from the form and proceeded to detail every place I had been during the trip. "No side trips to any Communist country in eastern Europe?" he asked. "Absolutely not," I replied. "I've never met a Communist in my life, at least not one that I knew about."

And that was it. I was excused by White Hat and walked out of Fort McNair, a free man and hopefully a future army intelligence officer.

It occurred to me later (lots of things occurred to me later) that this pair of military gumshoes had wasted their efforts on a scared, stupid little college student. Clearly their background investigation had turned up the fact that I had gone to Europe. Instead of dribbling away everyone's time and energy on a white- and black-hat show, they simply could have asked me about the trip. I would have answered honestly, and if I didn't, *then* they could try out some of their tricks. I tend to believe, too, that the humming box was a prop, not a real lie detector.

The background investigation (called a BI) was exhaustive; I knew that. Even before the battle of Fort McNair, my next-door neighbor had told me that some men, who identified themselves as MI agents, came to his door and asked personal questions about me.

"Does Eric like girls?" one of them asked.

"He likes girls too much, if you ask me," my neighbor said, probably remembering all the times he saw me pawing my dates in parked cars in front of my house.

Still, it was nice to know that the army cared about my social life and my moral qualifications for commissioning. It was nice to know that being a normal, hormone-crazed teenage sex maniac made me fit to be a second lieutenant. This is in almost amusing contrast to the way vice-presidents of the United States seem to be picked, i.e., late-night telephone calls from an exhausted presidential nominee during the heat of a convention and hasty security checks. But lowly junior officers—hey, *they* have to be pure.

Shortly before graduation and commissioning, I received my orders for active duty. I was scheduled to begin training by attending an infantry officers' basic course at Fort Benning, Georgia, and then MI branch school at Fort Holabird in Baltimore, Maryland. Beyond that, the army would not reveal what it had in mind for me, but I knew further orders would come later in the training cycle.

The problem was that my orders said I was to start at Fort Benning in October, four months after graduation in June. This was completely unacceptable. I was itching to go into the army, earn some decent money for the first time in my life, and get on with my two-year hitch. I didn't want to sit around in civilian limbo until the fall. Since I was supposed to be a future intelligence officer, I decided to find out exactly who had issued my orders and ask that person or persons to move my active-duty date to an earlier month, say July or August. I had always been told that it was impossible to change orders once they had been "cut," but I was desperate.

I checked with the army ROTC military science office at Georgetown, and good old Sergeant Blineberry told me they were issued from some obscure assignments office at Fort Meade, an army post in the Maryland suburbs of Washington. I borrowed my roommate's car, a 1957 Ford bomb, and sped out to Fort Meade shortly before lunchtime on the day I received the unsatisfactory orders. Starting with the gate guard, I kept inquiring all over the post until someone finally directed me to a leftover World War II

Quonset building sitting by itself at the edge of a grove of trees.

"There's a little old lady in there who writes all the active-duty orders for ROTC cadets on the East Coast," my last informant said.

I looked through the window; sure enough, a little old lady (she was probably in her early fifties, but that was ancient to me at twenty-one) sat at a battered metal desk, just beginning to eat her lunch. Everyone else had apparently left to eat elsewhere. I drove away to find someplace that sold flowers, and bought a dozen roses. When I returned, I walked quietly to the little old lady's desk and placed the roses on it.

"Hi," I said, "I wonder if you could let me into the army early." Then I explained who I was and specifically what I needed. I also begged a little, I guess, and tried to appear both eager to fight the enemy and pathetic at the same time.

"You know," she said when she had agreed to give me a July entry date, "I never get to see the young men I send these orders to. You're the first one who ever visited me, and you're certainly the first to bring me flowers."

I was a little skeptical that she was actually the person who could single-handedly alter my orders, but I figured all I had to lose was the price of a bunch of flowers. She must indeed have been the order-giver, because I received a new assignment to begin training at Fort Benning in late July. I was all set.

# CHAPTER 2

---

# Training Days

Graduation from Georgetown came soon enough. The day after I received my bachelor of arts degree, June 6, 1967, I was commissioned as a second lieutenant in the United States Army. My mother pinned the slender gold bars on my shoulder epaulets, and I just about burst out of my uniform with pride. As the commissioning class marched off the athletic field where the ceremony had been held, a crowd of students and teachers stood by with anti-war protest signs. They were eerily silent and shouted no slogans or epithets. In the crowd were a couple of girls I had dated. It was an unsettling reminder that I was entering a world and a country where being a military man, probably headed for service in Vietnam, was not considered an honorable thing to be or do. At that time, however, that mattered little to me. I was ready to be a grown-up, ready for some adventure, and the army certainly looked like it was going to give me plenty of that. I had no "political" opinions for or against the war in Vietnam or any other issues, for that matter. Ideologically, I was dumb and innocent.

I spent the next six weeks or so in a state of suspended animation. I lived in a rented apartment in Knoxville, Tennessee, where my girlfriend was trying to finish up at the University of Tennessee in time to marry me later in the year. It was an idyllic, yet still slightly melancholy, period for me. I was enjoying the last pleasures of civilian freedom. For the next two years, my soul as well as my ass would belong to the army.

In late July, I reported to Fort Benning in western Georgia and promptly saluted the first enlisted man I saw. Being a shiny new second lieutenant, I guess I could be excused for not recognizing all the uniform variations I would encounter. To me, this fellow standing near the training company office entrance looked like a general or at least a full colonel: pressed khakis, shined shoes, and a big gold eagle on his sleeve. So I saluted him.

"You don't have to salute *me*, sir," he said. "I'm supposed to salute *you*."

Seeing my confusion, and obviously having previous experience with first-day-of-active-duty chicken lieutenants, he explained that the eagle sewn on his sleeve was *not* the eagle of a full colonel (smaller, silver, and worn on the collar), but the more humble one of a specialist, fourth class, a rank well below mine.

Then he laughed out loud and threw me a contemptuous salute.

The infantry officer basic course at Fort Benning, home of the infantry branch, was designed to supplement the seven-week ROTC summer training camp I had attended between my junior and senior years. Our instructors never seemed to tire of reminding us that the infantry was the "queen of battle," and wisecrackers in the ranks never seemed to tire of saying, "Yeah, that's because she's always getting fucked by the king."

When I finished, I would be fully qualified in the army's eyes to lead a rifle platoon into combat. In my own eyes, obscured by thick army-issue glasses, I was no more competent to lead men into battle than a high-school cheerleader. This whole matter of infantry training, in fact, puzzled me until I reached Vietnam. If I was going to be an intelligence officer—presumably a calm, intellectual calling—why was it necessary for me to learn "irrelevant" things like rifle marksmanship, how to treat a sucking chest wound, and the best method of breaking an enemy sentry's neck from behind?

The answer is based on the old saying, "It takes one to know one,"' and here's how it works. Army branches in the 1960s were broken into three categories: combat, combat support, and support. The combat branches of infantry, armor, and artillery were supported, of course, by all of the other branches in every way possible—the man in battle had first claim on the army's resources. Pure support branches like judge advocate general, transportation corps, quartermaster, and adjutant general performed necessary and valuable services, but ones fairly well removed from combat (at least in most cases).

Combat support branches—like MI—were closer to the action. Their members frequently came under fire, and their services to the combat branches were often provided right on the battlefield. Since the basic mission of MI was to tell the infantryman about his enemy, the MI officer needed to know what kind of information was most useful to the man in the field. One of the best ways for an MI officer to learn this is to train first to be an infantry officer—to share the infantryman's conditioning, abilities, frustrations, and knowledge—and *then* learn the specific skills of an intelligence officer.

This was the reasoning behind my assignment to infantry school at Fort Benning, and fundamentally, I didn't disagree with it. In Vietnam, I found my infantry background to be useful in a hundred different ways every day, particularly when I was interrogating VC and NVA infantrymen and passing the information to U.S. infantrymen.

Nine hot, sleepless weeks later, I finished at Fort Benning and drove all night in a carful of fellow MI lieutenants to my next temporary post at Fort Holabird. On the way, we happened to pass through Annapolis, Maryland, which had served as the state capital since the eighteenth century. This small, charming city seemed like such a refuge from the army world I was sealed into that I silently promised myself to go back there one day, perhaps to live. Five years later, in the summer of 1972, I returned to take up what I hope today is permanent residence in Annapolis.

Fort Holabird, located in a bleak industrial neighborhood of Baltimore called Dundalk, was the home of the MI branch in the 1960s (in the 1970s it was moved to the Sunbelt post of Fort Huachuca, Arizona). It was there that presumably we would be initiated into the arcane rituals, customs, and operating procedures of military intelligence.

The course lasted only about a month, however, and I found too much of it to be disappointingly irrelevant to my assignment to Vietnam.

We sat in closed classroom buildings day after day, watching poorly produced slide shows and listening to lectures intended to familiarize us with the purposes, organizational structures, and techniques of our craft. The first thing we learned was the difference between information and intelligence—and the difference in our branch between those who simply collected information, and those who turned it into intelligence by analyzing it. I could tell right away that I was destined to dwell at the bottom of this figurative food chain: A combat intelligence officer, that is, a graduate of the MI branch Basic Course at Fort Holabird, was by definition only a generalist. He might be qualified to collect data from a variety of human and/or electronic sources, but the transformation of that raw data into assessments of enemy capabilities and intentions would be reserved for higher-ups with either more rank or more extensive training. Fort Holabird was just a boot camp for MI.

As the beautiful autumn days went by outside, we studied the "intelligence cycle"—how the essential elements of information (EEI) a commander needs to know are developed, collected, reported, disseminated, analyzed, and finally applied. From a progression of seemingly endless line-of-block charts, we learned the basic organization of both civilian and military intelligence agencies in the U.S. and around the world, especially those in the Communist bloc.

We were introduced, but only sketchily, to the functions of various component parts of our branch—counterintelligence, image interpretation, electronic surveillance, and technical intelligence (examining foreign equipment and material). We were issued copies of the basic MI bible, the FM 30-5 field manual, and told to commit most of it to memory. We were taught the fearfully strict set of rules about handling and protecting classified documents, and told all about confidential, secret, and top-secret clearances granted to people at different levels of the intelligence community.

We also studied the ways MI had prepared to support the army's effort in Vietnam. I never did master the complexities of the MI organizational structure there, but I did understand that combat divisions (and some independent brigades) had their own military intelligence detachments operating under the command of the 525th Military Intelligence Group headquartered in Saigon. In Saigon, too, were the Combined Military Interrogation Center, the Combined Document Exploitation Center, and the Combined Material Exploitation Center—facilities designed to coordinate the work of intelligence units around Vietnam and to provide information and intelligence on the strategic level. At that point in the war, my branch assigned officers down to divisions and, in some cases, their subordinate brigades, but no lower than that. Smaller units like battalions and companies usually gave intelligence duties to staff officers from other branches, usually the infantry, and they were called S-2 officers. Later, when I served with a brigade in Vietnam, I would be the only officer in the base camp wearing MI insignia on his collar.

My hopes of learning the more adventurous tricks of my chosen trade, like lockpicking, microfilming valuable enemy documents and seducing gorgeous foreign agents were dashed, however. The courses at Fort Holabird were straightforward and decidedly unexciting.

By this time, I had received orders that would take care of the rest of my pre-Vietnam training regime. Apparently because I had scored well on the language test back at Georgetown, I was assigned now to a nine-month course at the army's Vietnamese language school at Fort Bliss in El Paso, Texas. The school was run by an outfit called the Defense Language Institute, whose main "campus" was in lovely Monterey, California. The El Paso facility, located at Biggs Field, a former air force installation on the grounds of Fort Bliss, was set up to handle the "overflow" of students who couldn't be squeezed in at Monterey. Some of my MI classmates at Fort Holabird were disappointed ("royally pissed off" is a more accurate phrase, but I try to keep this account as free of excess profanity as possible) that they were being banished to the tumbleweed wastes of West Texas. They would much rather have spent their last

Stateside months on the picturesque coast of the Monterey Peninsula.

This wasn't going to happen. The army had finally realized it couldn't fight a war in Vietnam without at least a few of its number being able to speak the language of Vietnam. So by 1967, a fast-growing number of officers and enlisted men, especially the ones involved in intelligence activities, were being shipped off to various language schools and training facilities for varying lengths of time to learn Vietnamese.

I was part of one of the first cohorts of MI officers with formal language training to arrive in Vietnam. When I got there, I found that the Americans' lack of ability to speak the language caused untold problems at all levels of command, but that story will be told in more detail later.

I loved the deserts of West Texas and southern New Mexico. The sun shone more than three hundred days a year, you could see forty miles in all directions, and the clean, dry air hovered at about 15 percent humidity. I was also newly married and treasuring every day I could spend with my wife until I had to go overseas.

Language school was exciting at first, a drag toward the end of nine months of intensive study. I never learned to speak with any great fluency, and my vocabulary was no more extensive than a nine-year-old kid's. But Vietnamese is, from a grammatical viewpoint, a basically simple language. It is monosyllabic, which means no long, complicated words like the ones found too often in German (technological terms are usually borrowed from the more sophisticated Chinese, and hyphenated with Vietnamese words). Best of all, Vietnamese verbs aren't conjugated— one word placed before the verb, *da*, signifies that everything in the sentence has taken place in a past time, and one word, *se*, indicates the future. Of course, with this system, there is no way to tell whether the action took place six thousand years ago or yesterday, tomorrow or next year, but the context usually clears this up. The process of converting Chinese and Vietnamese characters to the Roman alphabet, which had been begun by French missionaries to Indochina several hundred years earlier, had been largely completed under French Colonial rule in the 1920s. I was pathetically grateful to those Frenchmen for making the language a lot easier for Westerners like me to read.

The problem with Vietnamese is not structure, but pronunciation. Like many Asian languages, Vietnamese is tonal, meaning that the same word can mean different things, depending on how the word is enunciated. Thus the word *ma* can mean "mother," "horse," or a host of other things (some of them embarrassingly profane) as it moves up or down the tonal scale. The five basic tones in Vietnamese are delineated with a set of diacritical marks that must be printed or typed above the vowels when a word is written. This became a serious matter when I got to Vietnam and began looking over lists of Vietnamese names and words typed by Americans who didn't know the language. But more about that later.

Another problem arose when I arrived at my first base camp in northern South Vietnam and tried to communicate with the locals. Most of the Vietnamese instructors at Fort Bliss had been from well-educated, economically comfortable families in the Saigon area. They spoke (and taught us) a precisely enunciated, high-class brand of Vietnamese that I found was nearly incomprehensible to the hardscrabble peasants of the countryside near my base camp. In the United States, it would have been like a New York City yuppie trying to speak with a semiliterate Arkansas redneck—the language was the same, but the accents were wildly dissimilar.

Graduation from the Defense Language Institute course came in late May 1968. I said good-bye to men I had been with as far back as Fort Benning (I would never see most of them again, although I heard later that all of my language school class had survived Vietnam), and used my final thirty-day leave to take a short vacation and move my wife back home to Knoxville, Tennessee, where she would be near her family while I went overseas.

My orders had arrived while I was in El Paso. I was assigned to the 635th Military Intelligence Detachment (MID) for the 23d Infantry Division, commonly known as the Americal Division (a nickname from World War II, when it was formed out of various leftover American units in New Caledonia). The division, composed of three infantry brigades and a huge headquarters element, was ensconced in a permanent base camp near the village of Chu Lai on the shore of the South China Sea in I Corps (U.S. forces in Vietnam were separated into Roman-numeraled tactical zones, numbered from I Corps in the north down to IV Corps in the Mekong River Delta), about sixty miles south of Da Nang. The MID to which I had been assigned, about forty people strong, was officially a subordinate unit of the 525th Military Intelligence Group at Tan Son Nhut near Saigon, but I would hear very little about that distant headquarters when I got to Vietnam. The MID focus was on the division it served, not some air-conditioned office hundreds of miles away. A good many of my classmates got assignments to the Combined Military Interrogation Center (CMIC) in Saigon, and I was jealous. They would be living in the relative comfort of a big city, while I was being exiled to the more primitive—and more dangerous—hinterlands.

My orders gave no indication of what my duties at the Americal MID would be. I was a marginally qualified infantry platoon leader, an MI branch officer with one month's branch training, and a barely functioning Vietnamese linguist. I was also an incompletely trained interrogator as a result of an MI correspondence course I had started, but never finished, while I was in language school. The interrogation course wasn't mandatory, but my classmates and I had been advised by some veterans at Fort Bliss that it would be good to take because Vietnamese linguists, even officers, were often used as POW interrogators in Vietnam. I assumed, therefore, that when I reached the Americal MID, I would automatically be assigned to the IPW (interrogation of prisoners of war) section there. Still, I was a fundamentally lazy person who was thoroughly enjoying the company of his new wife as well as the relaxed school schedule in El Paso, so I never troubled to continue the correspondence course after only a few lessons. The army didn't seem to care, so I didn't either. Later I would regret that.

# CHAPTER 3

# Chu Lai

Sometime around 12 July 1968, I climbed off the back ramp of a C-130 cargo plane and looked around me. It was over 120 degrees in the direct sun. I was standing at the far end of a runway of the Americal Division airfield in Chu Lai.

Through the heat waves shimmering off the macadam, I could see mottled green mountains to the west and a hint of blue-green South China Sea to the east. Low pine trees and sandy scrubland formed the rest of the visible horizon. As the C-130 spun around on its landing gear and taxied away, I thought to myself that this was the most alien, isolated, desolate spot I would ever see on earth.

Later that day, an orderly directed me into the office of the Americal military intelligence detachment, a one-story wooden hootch (all small buildings were called hootches) set with others just like it around a dusty parade ground in the center of the division administration area. I was immediately shown into the office of the MID commander, Major Zickle. He was a scholarly-looking man in early middle age who would be finishing up his tour in Vietnam soon. He made the usual welcoming comments, remarked on the heat, and then asked me what I wanted to do while I was at the MID.

This took me aback. I had assumed that I was needed to fill a specific duty slot there. I thought that my background, training, and rank had been considered carefully by the powers-that-be back in Washington at the MI Office of Personnel Operations, and that my assignment within the

Americal intelligence detachment was already decided. Perhaps Major Zickle was just trying to be polite, but he gave me the impression in his office that sweltering afternoon that I could simply pick my own assignment. This didn't square at all with the normal army practice of ordering people around. I was actually getting a *choice*.

"Well, sir," I said in a stumbling voice, "I sort of thought I would be working at the IPW section, doing interrogations or something like that. I took the Vietnamese language course at Fort Bliss, so I guess I should use it here."

"That's fine with me, Lieutenant Smith. You can start over at IPW as soon as you finish at the combat center."

And that was that. I was driven a couple of miles south to an area on the fringe of the Chu Lai base camp called the Combat Center. This cluster of shabby hootches and outdoor classrooms had been set up to give incoming soldiers a week of "in-country indoctrination" before they were assigned to line units. This included instruction on Americal Division organization and procedures, half-hearted reminders of the Geneva Convention rules, and tips on specialized tactics for that sector of I Corps. It also gave us a chance to acclimate ourselves to South Vietnam's ferocious heat and humidity. Living and learning conditions were primitive even by army standards, but I made a few friends there and picked up necessary information about my new division. When my time at the center was up, I was driven to the IPW section headquarters to report in for duty.

The IPW compound, as I viewed it for the first time from the front seat of an open jeep, looked like a relatively pleasant and orderly place. It was located between the eastern side of the Chu Lai airstrip and the South China Sea coast. The wide, bone-white beach nearby stretched up and down the shoreline as far as the eye could see. Except for the rolls of barbed concertina wire and the sandbagged guard bunkers, it could have been any resort beach in Florida or Bermuda. Clumps of pine trees sat around the sandy compound, lending an odd touch of cool New England to the broiling tropical landscape.

The dozen-odd buildings in the IPW area were standard army-built hootches, one- and two-room cabins with corrugated metal roofs, plywood siding, and screened windows. Some rested on low stilts, and all were rimmed with thick sandbag walls. Because the IPW section compound was built over spongy beach sand, all the buildings were connected with walkways made of grill-like bomb racks cadged from the Air Force. Bathrooms were wooden shower huts, three-holer latrines, and "piss tubes," metal cylinders driven down into the sand and covered at the top with screening. Although you couldn't exactly call it a pretty sight, the IPW compound sitting there on sand dunes overlooking the ocean had a neat, businesslike look about it.

In any case, it would be home for quite a while.

I was given a few days to settle into the unit's routine before I began doing interrogations. I inherited a .45 service automatic and scuffed holster from a lieutenant who was rotating home to the World (which was what we called the United States—the implication being that Vietnam was somehow not of this world) and his half of the tiny junior-officers' hootch. I met the IPW commander, Captain Powell, and Lt. Tom Guggenschaffer, the lively, fast-talking executive officer. The unit included one other officer, Lt. Seth Buttroon. A slight, wimpy young man, he was an artillery forward observer who, by some great stroke of fortune, had been accidentally detached to the IPW section when he arrived in country. Rumor had it that artillery FOs, whose job it was to direct cannon fire onto the enemy from close in, survived for only thirty days out in the field. Buttroon had every reason to be grateful for duty in our (relatively) safe base camp, and even more reason to be afraid that the artillery branch might discover its assignment error someday. As a result, he was constantly nervous, overly cautious about following orders, and obsequious toward superior officers. In other words, he seemed to kiss a lot of ass. We never got along, Seth and I, mainly because I was a natural-born breaker of rules and rude questioner of all orders, army procedures, and chickenshit regulations. I was also never in danger, like Seth, of being yanked from the IPW section and flown out to a rice paddy where I might get shot, so it was easier for me to display some moxie.

IPW had a roster of about twenty enlisted men who performed interrogations and administrative tasks. Many of these men were actually trained in interrogation techniques, which put them one up on me, the correspondence school dropout. Located right next to our compound was a small ARVN (Army of the Republic of Vietnam—our allies) intelligence unit that provided us with document translators and interpreters for POW interrogations.

After a few days, I was supposedly ready to conduct my first interrogation of a real live enemy prisoner. I don't remember this loss of my IPW virginity very well because it came on the heels of a rush of new experiences and impressions, but a few parts of it still stand out in my mind. On the morning of the interrogation, I took my clipboard full of notepaper and question formats over to the POW cage, which was conveniently placed near the IPW compound. As a temporary holding area, the cage was fitted out with only the barest essentials of incarceration—administrative hootch, barbed-wire fencing, a few guard towers, and thatched huts around an open plot of dust where prisoners were allowed to gather. The Americal Division cage was operated by the military police branch, although a number of the guards were simply former infantrymen waiting around to rotate home in a few months or weeks.

I asked around and was eventually directed to a group of about five miniature hootches (about thirty square feet) where prisoners were questioned. Contrary to what later press stories led people back in the World to believe, these interrogation facilities were not fitted out with chains, tongs, or fiendish electrical torture devices. Just a battered army-issue table and a few chairs. I sat down with the Vietnamese interpreter who had been assigned to me—neither the army nor I trusted my ability to speak the language yet—and waited for the prisoner to arrive under MP escort. I was expecting somebody big, mean and threateningly Oriental—someone on the order of Dr. No from the James Bond films or the evil, snarling Japanese concentration camp commander who chilled my blood in all those World War II movies.

The prisoner who arrived, however, was a skinny little bag of bones, with bad teeth and a dazed look in his eyes.

He was sporting the latest Viet Cong fashions: khaki shirt, black pajama pants, and Ho Chi Minh sandals made of pieces of castoff U.S. rubber tires. These sandals proved to be so durable and comfortable, though, that most of us at IPW adopted them as our footwear of preference both off and on duty. The fellow's glassy-eyed look came from a recent close encounter with several five-hundred-pound bombs dropped from U.S. B-52 aircraft flying at about forty thousand feet over the jungle trails of Vietnam. These attacks were code-named Arc Light strikes, and by all indications, they were America's most devastating, demoralizing weapon over there. Prisoners reported that they would be marching contentedly down the Ho Chi Minh trail when suddenly the whole world around them would erupt into a fireball, leaving craters twenty-five yards across and body parts everywhere. They had no warning and no escape. Many of the VC and NVA prisoners we saw had suffered severe hearing loss from having their eardrums shattered by the bomb concussions. I witnessed an Arc Light strike from several miles away one time and it looked and sounded like the hammer of God had struck the earth.

I knew these things about my prisoner from his "capture tag," literally a tag attached to his uniform or part of his body that contained information about the circumstances of his capture. This tag, almost more than any other piece of information, determined whether the prisoner would be ultimately released or sent to a permanent prison camp. No matter what they told us under interrogation about how innocent they were, if they had been caught shooting at Americans or ARVNs or even carrying a weapon, they were going to jail for the duration. The tags were usually filled out by an officer of the capturing unit, and some of the comments written onto the tag in scratchy ballpoint pen or pencil were emotionally revealing. "This fucking gook was taking potshots at us from a village tree line" would be one comment, or "This S.O.B. dink wounded two of my men with an AK-47," or "Prisoner was found in uniform, with a gun in his hand, running away from U.S. troops—we think he might be VC."

(A note here about Vietnam terminology. Americans called all Vietnamese, enemy soldiers or otherwise, "dinks," "gooks," "slopes," or "zips." Some of these words, like gook and slope, probably came from the Korean War veterans who were still on active duty in the late 1960s. The word zip stood for "zipperhead," a rather vague racial slur directed at the appearance of the Vietnamese. The word dink, which was used most frequently in my area of I Corps, derived from the Vietnamese word *"dien kia dau"* (often mispronounced by U.S. troops as "dinky-dow"), which meant "crazy." Presumably one had to be crazy to fight big, well-armed, and well-supplied American forces, but the emaciated, diseased VC who lived for weeks on rice carried in a sock proved they weren't so crazy, after all.

This particular prisoner was clearly VC. Guilty as hell, the tag said. He had been captured by one of the division's maneuver battalions during a heavy contact (army lingo for skirmishes and short-term battles) with elements of a full-time Main Force VC unit. Equipped with the list of required questions, called essential elements of information, I had been provided with for the interrogation, I looked the little guy in the eye and said, *"Nem gi?"* ("What is your name?").

*"Nem gi?"* repeated my interpreter, an ARVN sergeant who was ironically named Minh. The man gave his name, something like Nguyen Van Dong.

*"Bao lao ong Viet Cong?"* I asked in slightly ungrammatical Vietnamese ("How long have you been a member of the Viet Cong?"). The prisoner stared at the table top, not answering.

*"Tieu-wi noi bao lao Viet Cong?"* screamed Sergeant Minh, leaning into the prisoner's face ("The Lieutenant says how long have you been Viet Cong, dummy?").

The prisoner finally mumbled an answer, and continued to mumble nearly incoherent answers to all of our questions for the next hour. It turned out that the subject of my very first interrogation was the dumbest, least educated Vietnamese human being born in this century. He seemed to have only the dimmest idea that he had even been captured, much less where he had been and what he had been doing before the Americans scooped him up. One big problem was maps. This VC had no concept of what a map was.

Even after I explained that the little colored lines on the pretty piece of paper represented geographic features, he didn't comprehend a scintilla of my meaning. I couldn't track his infiltration route or locate his base camp if he couldn't tell me by using a map, so the interrogation was a total flop. *"Khong viet"* ("I don't know") was his standard answer to almost every query. I would hear that same phrase from many, many other prisoners over the next year, the stupid ones and the lying ones.

Sergeant Minh tried to explain that many VC were ignorant young peasants who could hardly read or write, but I had a difficult time reconciling this with my army-indoctrinated image of the crafty, jungle-wise enemy soldier. After a few more desultory questions and answers, I picked up my clipboard and called it quits. Minh was sympathetic, but he was also probably chuckling to himself about the ill-prepared greenhorn MI officers being shipped over to his country these days.

Later, as I was writing a report that attempted to sum up the useless information I had gleaned from my first IPW interview, I had a startling realization: *I couldn't tell if the prisoner had been lying or not.* My delayed reaction to this apparently simple insight hit me like a fist. I ripped my report and all five carbons out of the typewriter and slumped back in my chair.

This was serious stuff. I was American; the prisoner was Vietnamese. We came from dramatically different cultures, with different attitudes, opinions, and levels of sophistication. More importantly, we came from cultures that signaled personal statements differently. If an American was lying to me, I could read it on his face and in his voice—upper-lip sweat, shifting eyes, stammering, and other signals I had learned from infanthood to recognize. But a Vietnamese? Did *he* lower his eyes when he was bullshitting someone? Did he shift around in his seat? Did he sweat and mumble in a trembling voice when he was trying to hide something? Could I even distinguish between a Vietnamese mumble and a Vietnamese normal tone of voice?

Oh boy, was I in trouble. Without these cultural signals to guide me, I had no built-in crap detector. Maybe I could rely on my interpreters to tell me when they thought prisoners were lying, but maybe not. I could use research and supplementary information from documents to help me judge a prisoner's veracity, of course, but nothing could ever replace the "instinct" members of the same culture use to figure out each other's truthfulness.

I knew at that moment that I had a hell of a lot to learn about this interrogation business. Language training, incomplete correspondence courses, and a few classes in Vietnamese history and culture notwithstanding, I would have to start from scratch. Eventually I would learn some tricks and pointers, but they would come to me only with experience and after many failures.

Welcome to the Vietnam War, greenhorn. Sharpen your pencil and start taking notes.

# CHAPTER 4

## Paper Chase

It was clear to me that I was not yet a very skilled interrogator. In fact, I was a lousy interrogator. Presumably time and experience on the job would improve my performance. Most of all I would need to watch other interrogators do their jobs so I could learn by observing. That's precisely what I planned to do the next day, but my plans were temporarily sidetracked by a new, unexpected assignment from Captain Powell.

"You know, Smith, we're supposed to have someone like you handling document exploitation," he said the next morning. "Go on over to the documents hootch and get up to speed on what you need to know. Speak with Private Hiller." I had absolutely no idea what he was talking about, but already I had gotten used to being addressed this way—in summary, oblique armyese that sounded like Serbo-Croatian to my ears. What in the world could "document exploitation" mean?

I walked a few yards across the sand from the headquarters hootch to the documents hootch, yet another long, low wooden building piled around with sandbags. Pvt. Larry Hiller was young (eighteen years old), goofy-looking and casually disrespectful toward green officers like me. He was also as dumb as mulch.

His job, he explained in nasal midwestern tones, was to receive captured enemy documents, wrap them into a bundle and ship them off to the Combined Document Exploitation Center in Saigon. As far as he was concerned, that was about it.

"Where do all these documents come from?" I asked. Strewn across his desk, which was made of long planks haphazardly nailed together and braced on wobbly legs, were several filthy stacks of paper. Some of the leaflets and notebooks lying there looked like they had been stained with blood. It turned out they were.

"Oh, I get 'em from prisoners mostly," he said. "But sometimes the grunts out in the field dig up caches of documents and send 'em back here."

Larry's "exploitation" of the documents under his control was perfunctory. He merely sorted through them, cleaning off some of the sand and miscellaneous crud, until they were assembled into neat little piles. Then, if something looked "important" to him, he might give it to one of the MID's Vietnamese interpreters to check over. They in turn would write out a short summary of the document's contents in blurry ballpoint ink and hand it back to Larry. If he was so inclined at that juncture, he might pass the summary on to higher authorities. And then again, he might not. It depended on his mood and his work load. Larry wasn't very bright, so it was obvious that the significance of many documents was escaping his low level of comprehension.

In short, the entire document exploitation process was a disgrace. It had been placed in the hands of an untrained, unmotivated young private who had no conception of the potential value of captured enemy documents and no ability to organize the masses of material he was receiving, He simply sent the stuff off to Saigon to let distant intelligence analysts worry about it. Further, what little information had been gleaned was being mishandled and probably ignored by higher authorities. My training, of course, had not prepared me much for this eventuality. Back at Fort Holabird I had been presented with the generalities of document exploitation but not its specifics. In fact, until Captain Powell ordered me over to that cluttered hootch, I had hardly thought about the proposition that enemy documents as well as prisoners could help the intelligence effort. But now I could see the potential there.

I thanked young Hiller for briefing me and told him I'd be hanging around for a few days until I got used to his processing system. Inside my head, however, I started to formulate other, bigger plans.

First, I poked around the MID office files for a while. Knowing that at one time or another, the army had issued a manual for every military activity under the sun, I searched for a manual on enemy document handling. The one I finally pulled out of a drawer was written to show non-Vietnamese speakers how to identify Viet Cong and NVA documents. That was a start. Besides, my Vietnamese was so weak, I wasn't sure I could read, or even identify, the simplest enemy document without help. My next step was to take an informal survey of the kinds of documents Americal troops were taking off prisoners and pulling out of the ground.

Some of the papers were in cheap canvas pouches and torn leather cases that had been given up by prisoners when they were captured. These were almost always official documents: orders, rosters, equipment lists, propaganda publications, reports of various kinds. Other papers were lying loose or gathered into packets wrapped with rubber bands. These were usually personal documents, like letters, photographs of loved ones, notebooks and, surprisingly, diaries. I say surprisingly because I had been told back at Fort Holabird that Viet Cong and NVA soldiers were forbidden to keep individual diaries for the very good reason that they could fall into American hands. A VC diary might, for instance, reveal information about morale, infiltration routes, names of officers, and unit designations. This kind of material could be quite useful to an interrogator seeking to employ information about a prisoner's family against him. This was being done in North Vietnam, where enemy jailors taunted and weakened the resolve of American POWs with reference to their wives and children back home.

Despite official warnings, the VC and NVA troops, nevertheless, all seemed to keep diaries, and detailed ones at that. Their entries, scrawled into shabby, tattered little notebooks with ruled pages, were in most cases devoid of useful or even interesting information, however. The diarists were, after all, young, poorly educated peasants or city kids whose scope of literary expression was narrow. Still, I noted that many soldiers added naive drawings of flowers and trees to their writings—a touching bit of artistry from an unexpected source. They were also fond of writing bits of poetry (sort of a Vietnamese version of haiku) in these notebooks, but they tended to finish off their efforts with decidedly unpoetic clumps of Communist dogma. One enemy trooper concluded a nice couplet about clouds with the statement "and like the angry rain cloud, I will shower bullets on the Americans because I am proud to be a devout believer in the principles of Party socialism." I didn't know whether such contradictory sentiments were included to placate the political officers who were assigned to most VC and NVA units or not. If so, it meant that their superiors were occasionally reading the diaries, and therefore tacitly approving of their existence. If not, it meant that we were dealing with highly motivated soldiers who actually believed in Communist teachings, however rudimentary their knowledge of such matters might be.

The depression I was beginning to feel while I sorted through these documents hit me hardest when I read through a letter from a girl in Haiphong to her NVA boyfriend in South Vietnam. She had enclosed a tiny photograph of herself. It showed a young woman with glossy dark hair and the high, wide cheekbones that made Vietnamese women look so beautiful to Western eyes, although her appearance was otherwise ordinary. In the letter she exhorted her lover to "win the war so you can come back to lonely me." My own wife was writing things exactly like that to me nearly every day. In the same packet was the diary of the soldier who had received the letter, and in it, he said he missed his girlfriend as much as she missed him, and that he planned to marry her. He also told of his intent to revive his father's ruined farm when the war was over.

The only problem here was that the soldier was dead, punctured with M-16 bullet holes two days before, during a firefight with American troops. His diary, the letter, and the picture were caked with swabs of dried blood. He would never work that farm, and I knew, long before his girlfriend did, that her young man wasn't ever coming home to her.

Indeed, the majority of documents I was examining were stained and spattered with mud, old blood, and who knew

what other bodily substances because they were retrieved
from dead or wounded soldiers or from their battlefield
graves. That accounted for the strange (but soon to be familiar) smell of the piles of documents in the office. It was
a sickly-sweet stench that never failed to unsettle me. I
learned from these documents, too, that there weren't any
important differences between my enemy and me. American media depictions of crafty, ruthless guerrillas
nothwithstanding, I now knew that Charlie (derived from
Victor Charlie in the army phonetic alphabet for VC) was
as human as I was. And just as miserable for a lot of the
same reasons. There was a certain pathetic—and
sympathetic—quality about these intimate diaries and letters
that moved me considerably. They were written by people
from a poor, largely rural society that couldn't even afford
to provide decent writing paper or notepads for its soldiers.
They were written by people with achingly limited ambi-
tions and prospects, but who still believed they could beat
the richest and most powerful nation in the world. The
irony is that they managed to pull it off, rustic peasant poetry and all.

Other documents in Larry Hiller's soiled, scattered stacks
could be taken less seriously. These were propaganda mate-
rials found in the possession of prisoners, and sometimes local villagers, when they were searched. I never could figure
out why a soldier, already burdened with pack and weapon,
would lug bundles of propaganda around, too, but I was
learning that the Southeast Asian mind was hard to fathom.
Perhaps the soldiers were part of a courier distribution network, or maybe they just intended to use the documents,
many of which were printed on flimsy rice paper, as toilet
paper. The propaganda was written in English, of course,
since it was directed at American troops, but in some cases
it employed a brand of English that could only be described
as "bozo pidgin." Here is a hilariously garbled sample from
the psychological warfare offices of the Quang Nam Province National Liberation Front (the Americal Division operated in Quang Nam, Quang Ngai, and Quang Tin provinces):

GIs! Let do as [President] Johnson has done or at least
you take part in the struggle movement of the American

people opposing the U.S. aggressive war in Vietnam by refusing the fight, demanding go home and not interfere on Vietnamese internal affairs.

Pretty persuasive, eh? And a model of grammatical eloquence, too. The same Quang Nam English scholar who composed that prose was also probably responsible for this crude but creatively heartrending appeal:

> Your blood have been shed too much, but Johnson have brought to you and American people? Shame— mourning and suffering. The US war maniacs have got use to live on your blood and bone. How can your lives be exchanged with payment or purple Heart if you go home a cripple or in a bag made by chemicals? Demand your repatriation.

You can see we weren't fighting an army of Shakespearean bards or UCLA grads. One group called the Central Trungbo Revolutionary Armed Forces even tried to exploit American racial turmoil by publishing a leaflet addressed to "US Armymen—Negro Armymen," advising them in reasonably accurate syntax (if not spelling) to "oppose the fasist acts of the US government" and "don't die in vein— BATTLEFIELD FOR YOUR TRUE FREEDOM."

Occasionally a document generated by more official sources offered amusing insights into the enemy's way of thinking about, well, certain sensitive subjects. Here is a Viet Cong staff memo on the role of whores in I Corps:

> It is well known that the dollar-fed Americans are more loquacious when they are with a woman, especially in mating, and the stupid brutes are likely to reveal information of a tactical nature. It is therefore incumbent upon us to ensure that the party girls transmit information to us, from the bedside if necessary.

Now that would be a good trick: hiding a radio in bed. If horny American GIs weren't more careful, they might go home in those "bags made by chemicals."

A few years after returning from Vietnam, I happened to

run across a slender paperback volume entitled *The Role of Military Intelligence* in a used-book store. It was written by Maj. Gen. Joseph A. McChristian, who had been Gen. William Westmoreland's assistant chief of staff for intelligence from 1965 to 1967. McChristian was the man, it turned out, who set up the entire information gathering and evaluation system that I became a part of in the summer of 1968. Although this reportlike Department of the Army publication was hardly what you'd call riveting reading, I did learn some interesting bits of history from it. In January 1966, for instance, General McChristian arranged for the Army of South Vietnam (ARVN) to assign "mirror" intelligence detachments of interpreters and document analysts to every corps and division-level U.S. unit in Vietnam. This ensured not only that the ARVN would be kept up to snuff on intelligence gathered by American forces, but also that American forces would enjoy the full benefit of having Vietnamese-speaking intelligence specialists on the spot to help out our MIDs.

In his book, General McChristian (who later went to the Pentagon to head up the army's entire military intelligence branch) said, "Indeed, units without Vietnamese support often contributed to the overload of the exploitation system by forwarding volumes of meaningless documents [to the Combined Document Exploitation Center in Saigon]." That is precisely what poor Larry Hiller had been doing until I got there. It apparently never occurred to him that somewhere nearby a fully staffed ARVN MID waited to help him with his piles of documents. The interpreters, tough ARVN sergeants who lived in the Americal MID compound and seldom even saw their bosses over at the ARVN MID office, either forgot to tell Larry about this or simply failed to volunteer the information if they weren't asked about it directly. The latter was more typical of our close-mouthed interpreters.

Now, after surveying Larry's defective processing methods as well as the variety of documents coming into MID hands, I knew how my work was cut out for me. I had to locate the ARVN MID somewhere in the base camp, enlist its help in getting at least a preliminary readout of these masses of documents, and then make sure that whatever useful information I got was quickly passed up to higher authorities. It was obvious, even to an FNG (fucking new guy—newcomer to Vietnam) like me, that captured documents had as much to tell us about the enemy as the prisoners we so carefully questioned.

# CHAPTER 5

# Changes

The next few weeks were sort of schizophrenic for me. I was dividing my time between sorting out the documents mess and trying to observe as many interrogations as I could fit in. At the division level, we were seeing prisoners who, in most cases, had already been screened and briefly questioned by military intelligence teams at the three infantry brigades attached to the Americal Division. These brigades, the 11th, the 198th, and the 196th, contained about three thousand men each and were spread over sixty miles of mountains, rice paddies, and coastal plains—one of the largest areas of U.S. responsibility in the country. The 11th Brigade, based near the village of Duc Pho, was approximately thirty miles south of Chu Lai, and the 196th Brigade, headquartered at Landing Zone (LZ) Baldy, was approximately thirty miles to the north of us. The 198th Brigade at LZ Bayonet, situated a couple of miles southwest of Chu Lai, functioned as the guard brigade for the division base camp in addition to conducting its own operations.

It was shortly after I arrived at Chu Lai that I learned about these brigade units, called military intelligence teams (MITs). In the summer of 1968, they were still independent operations run like little feudal kingdoms by lieutenants who were not yet under the direct command of the division MID. They could be tasked for specific purposes and operations by the MID commander, in this case Major Zickle, but generally speaking they were free to run things on their own. By December these teams, usually made up of about

36

a dozen interrogators and counterintelligence agents, would be brought into the official fold when the Americal Division restructured itself into a unified, centralized force. The present disarray was due to the fact that the Americal had landed in Vietnam two years before as Task Force Oregon, a rather loose association of combat units that spread out along the coast south of Da Nang to deploy against the NVA and VC working the area. As time went on, the Americal brass brought first the infantry brigades, then combat support units like the MIDs under a single command structure.

That was still months away, however, and I would play an uncomfortable (and almost fatal) part in that reorganization. Meanwhile, I looked at the brigade intelligence team chiefs as romantic, swashbuckling figures. These cocky young officers would show up at Chu Lai on business once in a while, dressed in sun-faded jungle fatigues and sporting exotic weapons on their nonregulation gunbelts. To emulate them one time, I bought a rakish, open-topped black leather holster and belt in the nearby village of An Tan. After a few weeks of constantly cleaning Vietnam's ubiquitous red dust off my corroding .45 pistol, though, I wisely went back to the plain but serviceable government-issue holster with its protective flap. I envied those team chiefs for their apparent freedom from the rigidity I was already finding so oppressive at division headquarters. They seemed to exist far out of reach of all the army chickenshit. The thought occurred to me that one day I might like to be one of them, although at the time, such an independent command was well beyond my experience or abilities.

The main part of the brigade MIT's job was to screen out any obviously innocent Vietnamese civilians and make preliminary inquiries of prisoners who were likely VC or NVA. Innocent villagers they simply released. Certified prisoners of war (POWs) were subsequently shipped up to division for a lengthier and more thorough interrogation. At division, we used the brigade interrogation reports, invariably sketchy due to the hurried conditions under which they were written (they were only allowed to retain prisoners for a day or two), as a basis for our own questioning. I learned more every day by watching veteran enlisted and officer interrogators do their jobs and by talking, sometimes in my halting Vietnamese and sometimes in English, with the ARVN interpreters assigned to us.

The question of whether a prisoner was lying or not was one I never completely resolved, but I did pick up a few pointers. The interpreter I got to know best, Sergeant Minh, a kindly, intelligent man somewhere in his thirties, told me that Vietnamese who lied frequently displayed the stress of it by digging their fingernails into the insides of their hands. Thus, if you examined their hands after a period of questioning, you could find evidence of untruth by looking for half-moon nail indentations on their palms. I tried this trick with mixed results over the next months. One problem was that all detainees were naturally under stress simply because they had been captured and thrown into a prison camp. At times they had been mistreated by their captors in the field. The presence of nail imprints didn't necessarily mean they were lying on a specific point, but as an overall indicator of veracity, it was still better than no clue at all. Another way to determine if an unclassified prisoner was, in fact, an enemy soldier was to examine the tip of his right index finger. If it showed a pattern of small, parallel cuts in the skin, it could mean he had recently been firing an AK-47 assault rifle, the standard shoulder weapon of VC and NVA forces— the AK-47 trigger was serrated along the forward edge and would make distinctive marks on the trigger fingertip.

During this period of apprenticeship, I also got to watch a master craftsman in action—Tom Guggenschaffer, the soon-to-be-going-home first lieutenant who had been the executive officer of the IPW section. Guggenschaffer was the kind of fast-talking, dog-robbing, wise-cracking bullshit artist you see in those classic Hollywood movies about World War II, the guy who can steal the treads off a German tank and bed a beautiful French girl at the same time. Only Guggenschaffer was real, and damn good at his job when he wasn't dating American nurses in Quang Ngai City or lolling on the South China Sea beach to improve his suntan. Despite his administrative duties, he frequently helped out with interrogations, and one night I saw him pull off an absolutely convincing bit of playacting. An enlisted interrogator was having trouble with a prisoner who refused to talk or even give his name and rank. The word was passed for Guggenschaffer, apparently to go through a familiar—but devastatingly effective—routine. He showed up outside the interrogation hootch five minutes later, red-faced and shouting at the top of his lungs. "Where is that fucking goddamn dink? I will shoot his balls off! Show him to me now!"

The prisoner couldn't understand a word of this, of course, but the alarming howls spewing from Guggenschaffer's mouth clearly boded no good for anybody within range. Tom then stormed into the little hootch, ostentatiously yanking back the cocking slide on his .45 automatic; he hauled the prisoner out of his chair and slammed him up against the wall. Suspending the now-terrified prisoner with one hand, he used the other to jam the pistol straight into the prisoner's mouth. "Talk, you little asshole or I'll blow your fucking face into rice pudding!" Or words to that effect. Not able to mistake Guggenschaffer's meaning, the prisoner talked. He babbled uncontrollably, in fact. He rambled on so much that ten minutes passed before he could be calmed down enough to make sense to his interrogator. Guggenschaffer then grandly made his exit.

Now that was real "guerrilla theater." Tom told me afterward that his outburst had of course been calculated down to the last threatening gesture. His pistol was unloaded, too, so nobody could be shot accidentally. Months later I tried this same ploy, copying Guggenschaffer's every intonation and movement—but with quite different results. That's another story, however.

I had by this point been in country long enough to know what I was in for. My life in Vietnam looked like it was going to consist of long periods of mental exertion, drudgery, and ennui that would suddenly be punctuated by an event so frightening it would make me wet my pants—what some veteran had once called "90 percent boredom and 10 percent terror." I had already endured my first midnight barrage when the local VC lobbed in a few 122mm rockets to remind us of their existence outside the base-camp fence. Along with everyone else in the IPW compound, I had awakened a microsecond after the first explosion and sprinted in record time to the closest bunker. There I pressed my face into the sand, stuck my fingers in my ears, and prayed for a few more minutes of existence. I also missed my wife unendurably and wished about every five minutes for any one of thousands of comforts of home I didn't have: a peanut butter and jelly sandwich, air-conditioning, a toilet that flushed.

But I also realized something else. Each morning while I shaved (often out of my helmet), for a few moments at least I was actually glad to be in Vietnam. It was, after all, the center of the world's attention at that time. I was not just watching, but participating in history as it was being made. I was on ground zero, unpleasant as that ground was. Leaving out questions of politics or liberal morality, I was sure that school classmates who had avoided military service would someday be sorry they missed this classic rite of passage for a young man. They were back in the World, living safe, normal lives while I was thinking of them (and envying them a little), but in truth, I preferred to be where I was, standing under a hostile, tropical sun. Since then I have read the scene in Shakespeare's *Henry V* that expresses this feeling with uncanny perception, especially for a nonveteran like Shakespeare. Just before the hungry, wet, outnumbered English army of archers goes out to meet the French at the Battle of Agincourt, Henry gives his men the pep talk that will speak to nervous soldiers trough the ages:

> This day is call'd the feast of Crispian.
> He that outlives this day and comes safe home
> Will stand a tip-toe when this day is named,
>
> . . . . . . . . . . . . . . . . .
>
> And gentlemen in England now a-bed,
> Shall think themselves accurs'd they were not here,
> And hold their manhoods cheap whiles any speaks
> That fought with us upon Saint Crispin's day.

July blended into August, and I became a first lieutenant by automatic fiat of the army. This was not a "promotion" in the usual sense because during the Vietnam years, a second lieutenant had to be either dead or criminally, unforgivably incompetent to avoid gliding up to the next rank, first lieutenant. Army tradition holds that you have to buy a drink for everyone in the officers club bar on the day of a promotion, but I merely went down to the PX that day and bought a couple of sets of silver bars. I pinned them on my collar and the front of my fatigue hat, and that was that. Even so, things began to change around the IPW compound. Captain Powell rotated home, and Lieutenant Guggenschaffer, who should have succeeded him as IPW section chief, repaired instead to the beach for the remaining weeks of his tour. It sort of devolved upon me to make small, and then larger, decisions about the day-to-day running of the unit. By the time Guggenschaffer left the Chu Lai airstrip on the freedom bird home, I was the senior lieutenant on site and, therefore, by process of elimination, the acting section chief.

I wasn't really prepared for this responsibility, and it showed. Although I managed to bluff my way through certain basic duties, I could never get used to dealing directly with higher-ranking officers. Whether he is a temporary section chief or not, a first lieutenant does not speak as an equal with captains, majors, and lieutenant colonels. Whenever I had to meet with them about IPW business, or handle their routine requests for prisoner information, I couldn't help behaving like a subordinate. As a result of my shyness, I had to eat a lot of shit from above. "Shit rolls downhill," the old army saying goes. The IPW enlisted men, too, knew that I was basically a green FNG who barely knew how to conduct an interrogation on my own. Reports got out on time, telephone calls were answered, POWs were processed through, files were filed—but I wasn't comfortable in Captain Powell's office chair. How uncomfortable was I? Well I sat in it only about an hour a day, in the morning. The rest of the time I hung out in the documents hootch, with my shirt off, trying to change Larry Hiller's chaotic habits and pretending I wasn't really in charge. Secretly, of course, I relished the role of commander, but I was also smart enough to realize that the sun needed to fade out my fatigues a little more before I could assume that role with authority. That day would come.

We had been hearing rumors that the IPW section was going to get a new boss, a captain being sent out from the States. The rumor solidified into a memo to me from the

MID commander saying that Capt. Rufus Steele would be arriving in the second week of August to take over the IPW section. I had mixed feelings about being supplanted like this—on one hand I was relieved to get all those demanding superior officers off my back, but on the other hand, I was starting to see myself sitting in Captain Powell's chair for an extra hour each morning.

On the afternoon Captain Steele arrived at the compound, I was, as usual, sweating away in the humid confines of the documents hootch. When I heard what was obviously his voice outside, talking to the interrogator who was showing him around, I pretended I didn't hear a thing. Like a spoiled child, I was going to sit on my resentment and let this FNG come to me. That was my first mistake in handling my relationship with Captain Steele.

# CHAPTER 6

# Locking Horns

The first meeting between Captain Rufus Steele, the incoming IPW section chief, and his lieutenant, the resentful, part-time former acting section chief, did not go well. I mumbled a sourpuss welcome to him, and he asked me abruptly why I hadn't greeted him the moment he arrived at the IPW compound—indeed, why hadn't I picked him up myself at MID headquarters and driven him back to show him around personally? I had no good answer to that. I was not only full of sour grapes about his supplanting me, but as a reserve officer with barely more than a year in service (and most of that in training schools), I was also ignorant of the most fundamental rules of active-duty courtesy. The thought of easing his passage into command of the IPW section simply never occurred to me, the same way it never occurred to me to buy a round of drinks at the officers club when I was promoted.

Steele grunted his disapproval, then ordered me to escort him on a tour of the compound. I did my best to act friendly after that, but it was only an act, and he could see it. Before ten minutes had passed, I knew in my heart that Steele had decided I was obnoxious, troublesome, and surly. Worse, I was a snotty, know-it-all, ROTC college kid in uniform who wasn't fit to spit shine the boots of an up-from-the-ranks hotshot like him (he had been a sergeant who won a battlefield commission on his last tour in Vietnam. This kind of officer was known as a mustang). Steele was right about two things: I was definitely a know-it-all, a character flaw that offends people to this day, and Steele was without question a hotshot. Throughout his tenure at the IPW section, he displayed all the classic leadership traits I had been taught to admire—decisiveness, toughness, and thorough knowledge of his job. Despite our personality clash, I thought him an excellent commander overall. He was wrong on two other points, however; despite my reserve commission and less-than-fanatical devotion to the army, I thought I had the makings of a competent, even skilled officer; I also held no grudge against him because of the source of his commission—quite the opposite, in fact. It seemed that Steele and I were destined to cordially loathe each other's guts from the moment we met. We got off on the wrong combat boot, so to speak. This would cause both of us a lot of problems in the future. Toward the very end, though, we came to understand and possibly even respect each other, and the story of how we got to that point will be told.

Meanwhile, I was formally evicted from my sometime seat at the IPW commander's desk; it was back to documents and interrogations for me. Even while functioning as the acting section chief, I had been sprucing up the documents process a little bit at a time. One thing I needed desperately to do was to find help with translating, or at least summarizing, the loads of documents before forwarding them on to Saigon. My quick review of the enemy papers in our possession had indicated to me that useful, important information—especially about the Americal's local area of operation—could be extracted from them (in his book, General McChristian said that at least 10 percent of documents captured on the battlefield contain information of intelligence value). By the time distant, unconcerned translators in Saigon got any of that information back to us, it could be obsolete.

So I started to ask around. Is there an ARVN intelligence detachment somewhere in the Chu Lai base camp? Am I allowed to ask this unit for help? How much help? Does this unit "do" documents? The answers were fast in coming—from the Vietnamese interpreters, experienced clerks at MID headquarters, and our own interrogators: "Sure, there's an ARVN MID just over that sand dune at the end of the IPW compound"; "Yes, of course, they'll be glad to handle document translations." So I put Larry Hiller happily to work sorting papers into labeled stacks and walked over to the ARVN headquarters hootch on the far slope of the sand dune.

The captain in charge there was pleasant and helpful (and polite about my botched Vietnamese). I needed only to send the documents over to him, and he would ensure they were looked at. Over diagrams roughed out on notepaper and a conversation in mutual pidgin English mixed with Vietnamese, we agreed that his document analysts (I never knew exactly how many there were. Sometimes he may even have called upon the services of our IPW interpreters, who officially belonged to him, after all) would exercise their own discretion in deciding which documents to translate completely. Others of lesser importance would be summarized on a page or two, and patently useless ones would simply be listed. If I spotted anything of interest to me, I could request in a note clipped to the document bundle that it be "read out" or translated in its entirety. No muss, no fuss. The system the ARVN captain and I arranged that day worked quite well thereafter. They got the information they wanted; they got to do the job they were sent to the Americal to do, and so did I. If any of it leaked out to the enemy through the ARVN MID, whose security procedures were beyond my control, I never heard about it. Besides, I was now in the document processing business for real.

My next step was to alert higher authorities that, henceforth, actual, live, current information about the opposition's troops and intentions in our area would be coming out of the IPW documents section regularly. Captain Steele would receive a copy of all readouts, of course, and then the MID commander. The order of battle (OB) shop—where information from all human and electronic sources was compiled into loose-leaf notebooks and marked on maps—would receive copies, too. In fact, anybody who cared to see what the enemy was saying in writing could see it, from the duty officer at the division's tactical operations center (TOC) to the assistant chief of staff for intelligence on the Americal commanding general's staff. The name of the game was widespread dissemination. Within the bounds of reason and MI security rules, naturally.

Here was the way my new, improved (post-Larry) system was going to work:

**1.** Scruffy, bloody enemy documents would be delivered in chaotic stacks and bundles to my desk in the documents hootch by interrogators or through evacuation directly from the field. The infantry routinely shipped captured documents back to us on supply helicopters each day; the bundles were usually, but not always, accompanied by a capture tag (like the ones attached to prisoners), listing the capturing unit as well as the date, place, and circumstances of capture.

**2.** I would go over the documents, employing my language-school–level Vietnamese and that document identification manual I had found in a file drawer. If anything looked interesting, I would make a note of it for the ARVNs.

**3.** The ARVN MID analysts would get the bundle from me within forty-eight hours. They would send back a document readout report after a few days. Because the ARVNs belonged to a different army with different ideas about efficiency, I tried to avoid setting any kind of deadline for their reports. When emergencies arose, as they did on occasion, I used our own interpreters for quick translations. The ARVNs performed reliably, however, and I don't remember having to wait more than four days for a normal-size bundle to be analyzed. Large shipments of documents took more time, of course, but even then it was seldom longer than a week.

**4.** After looking over the translations and summaries, I selected documents that merited special attention for one reason or another. Some of them might mention an upcoming attack on a U.S. base camp or an ARVN installation, for instance. Others might reveal the names of ranking NVA officers or VC infrastructure members (infrastructure was our name for the political side of the Viet Cong—the "shadow government" it maintained alongside the regular South Vietnamese government agencies and administrative subdivisions). Whatever I considered important, informative, or just interesting, I had translated completely by the ARVN MID or our interpreters and then issued a spot report on it. These spot reports were radioed to Saigon, of course (Saigon was very nosy and always wanted to know what was going on everywhere in Vietnam), and to offices in the Americal intelligence community.

**5.** Finally, I wrapped each day's quota of document bundles in two thick layers of brown package-paper, tied the parcel with a few yards of string, addressed it to the Combined Document Exploitation Center (CDEC) in Saigon, and drove to the army post office at base camp headquarters to mail it off. Postage was free, thank God. To this day, thanks to all the practice I got, I am a whiz at wrapping postal parcels so securely the recipients need a hacksaw to open them.

Before I actually got my jiffy five-step process going, I personally visited the offices of all the people I thought might be interested in document information to tell them it would soon be forthcoming. I told them that from then on they could rely on a continuous stream of information from this previously intermittent source. Captain Steele was the only one who didn't act impressed. He felt that somebody should have been doing this all along and that it shouldn't have taken a concerted effort to process documents as efficiently as prisoners were; he hadn't been in charge very long and had no idea of what a sloppy state the documents office had been in before I was so casually assigned to it by his predecessor.

But Steele was right, of course. All this should have been done by someone long ago, and all I did was reorganize it up to a minimum level of acceptability. The only excuse that could be offered was that the Americal Division MID was still in flux, as were the rest of the division's support units. Even so, I felt my first twinges of pride in doing a job the way it ought to be done. After four years of ROTC and another year of training, it was nice to accomplish something concrete in the "real" army.

A day or two after I settled into my new document routine, another problem came to my attention, and it was one I wasn't permitted to ignore. I found out that the Americal Division's blacklist, so carefully assembled over two years, was almost completely useless.

# CHAPTER 7

# Echoes

First, a little deep background on the blacklist disaster.

Sometime after it had committed several hundred thousand troops to Vietnam, a country with which the United States had had few dealings, the army suddenly realized that quite a large number of its troops and even senior officers couldn't speak a word of Vietnamese. This, as anyone could see, was not a happy situation. It meant that U.S. forces would continually be forced to rely on ARVN allies for even the simplest tasks—like getting directions to the nearest latrine, finding out where the enemy might be hiding, and in the case of our intelligence effort, finding out what the devil the enemy was saying in the first place. The ARVN forces were, of course, riddled with VC spies, part-time agents, double agents, and assorted Communist sympathizers. It simply wouldn't do to rely too heavily on our South Vietnamese brothers for information we ought to be obtaining for ourselves.

Thus was born the army's Vietnamese language training program, or at least that's what I was told at MI basic school in Fort Holabird and again at the Defense Language Institute school in El Paso. I was given to understand that I was part of one of the first cohorts of MI officers to be instructed in the Vietnamese language, and as such I had a duty to use my skills to the fullest once I arrived in country. My instructors said I should be on the lookout for any way in which I could be useful as a Vietnamese speaker because, in 1968 at least, there weren't a whole hell of a lot of us over there. At Fort Holabird they emphasized this with two versions of a documentary film shot the year before during a meeting in Vietnam between an American senior officer and a local village chief who was friendly to our side. The U.S. officer used an interpreter to speak with the village chief, and in the first version of the film, here is how it went:

Officer to interpreter, "Ask the chief what his feelings are about the American troops he has met. Are they treating him and his fellow villagers well?"

The interpreter then speaks in rapid Vietnamese to the village chief for about thirty seconds.

Village chief to interpreter, in a loud voice and with clenched fist waved in the air, *"Mot hai ba buon nam shau bay tam chin muoi!"*

Interpreter to officer, "I'm sorry, but he says the American troops are ruining his village and mistreating the people there. He says that the U.S. President Johnson is an evil running dog who is trying to destroy his country."

Well, it turned out that this was all a setup. U.S. intelligence had reason to believe that the interpreter was working for the VC, so they filmed—and also secretly sound-recorded—his little conversation with the village chief. Later, when a trusted Vietnamese interpreter told the Americans what the suspected interpreter had actually been saying to the village chief, the worst suspicions were confirmed. Back at Fort Holabird, we got to see the second version of the film, too, this time with a complete translation of what the interpreter really said:

Officer to interpreter, "Ask the chief what his feelings are about the American troops he has met. Are they treating him and his fellow villagers well?"

Interpreter to village chief, "Listen, you old fool. I am VC, and after the Americans leave, I am going to come back here and punish you if you don't do and say exactly as I tell you. Now, you will count from one to ten in a loud voice and throw your fist in the air after each number. Now do it!"

At this point the poor, intimidated village chief did as he was told. The words *Mot, hai, ba, boun, nam, shau, bay, tam, chin, muoi* are nothing more than the numbers one through ten in Vietnamese. The interpreter then made up his own translation of what the chief had said to trick the U.S. officer into believing that the locals hated Americans and their "evil running dog" of a president.

This film was persuasive, to say the least. All of us watching it realized that our ability to speak Vietnamese would be of immense value in many situations over there, especially during interrogations. When I got set up at the Americal MID, therefore, I kept my eyes open for ways to use it. My chance came soon enough.

The heat was oppressive as I sat in my documents office (indeed my only office) typing up a report from that morning's interrogation of a minor official in the VC-sponsored "farmers association," a sort of political support group for local-yokel village Communists. As I say, the heat was awful, neverending. I had to insert a leather patch under my wristwatch to keep the metal back from corroding away with my constant sweating. My wallet had to be wrapped in plastic sheeting to protect it from the sweat pouring off my butt and into my back pocket. When I wrote letters home, I had to fix a towel to my sweating forearm with rubber bands so the ballpoint ink wouldn't smear. That summer in Vietnam the temperature went well over one hundred degrees nearly every day, and humidity made the air sag. I was always bathed in my own moisture,

During the interrogation earlier, I had routinely asked the detainee to name some of his colleagues in the farmers association. This question came from the EEI (essential elements of information) list I carried into every interview. The list contained about twenty-five basic questions that had to be asked of each prisoner, things like name, unit, unit infiltration route, names of officers, types of weapons, knowledge of the unit's future plans and travel routes, hospital locations, weapons cache locations—the usual questions that probably have been asked of military prisoners since organized warfare began. Occasionally the EEI list would be updated and supplemented with questions of more current interest. I remember that for a while we asked every ragtag VC and NVA trooper if he knew anything about Red Chinese forces entering the war (probably a leftover but nevertheless powerful fear from the Korean War). Another question, this one of intense interest to me because of my personal fears, concerned detainees' knowledge of American POWs anywhere in the Americal zone. Some prisoners reported seeing tall white men out in the jungle, but they couldn't tell us if they were Americans or Russian advisers. All round-eyes looked alike to them, I guess.

In any case, my cooperative prisoner rattled off a few farmers association names in reply to my question. I duly wrote the names down and transferred them to my typewritten interrogation report. Squinting through the sweat balls rolling down my forehead, however, I dimly realized something was wrong. It was the names. What about the names? Oh, yes, I had forgotten to add the all-important pronunciation marks to them. One of the first lessons I had learned in language school was that without these diacritical marks Vietnamese words can sometimes be scrambled. A world like *nha*, so simply spelled, could mean any one of a half-dozen things, from "house" to "white," depending on which of five pronunciation symbols appeared over the vowel. I immediately went back to into the cage and got the prisoner to write down the names in his scrawly, semi-literate script so I could put them in my report. These would then be added to the blacklist kept by MID's counterintelligence (CI) section. At some future time, either a CI team or a U.S. infantry unit would enter a village and be able to round up infrastructure members using these names. This was the function of the blacklist, a file cabinet full of cross-referenced Vietnamese names kept at the CI office under strict security.

I saw the problem as soon as I returned to my typewriter. I couldn't very well type the names with an American-made machine because it had no keys for the diacritical marks. The only typewriters I knew of equipped with special keys like that were over at the ARVN MID, and the ARVNs never lent them out to us. So how were correctly marked names getting onto the CI blacklist from incorrectly equipped American typewriters? Uh, oh.

A fast walk over to the CI office, located in a grove of pines at the west end of the IPW compound, led me to the blacklist file cabinet. Riffling through the folders I saw right way that we had, in the words of Paul Newman from the movie *Cool Hand Luke*, "a failure to communicate." All the blacklist names were typed without diacritical marks. To get some idea of what this meant, imagine walking into Chicago and asking for everybody named Kowalski to step forward. Or go to San Francisco's Chinatown and ask to speak with all the people named Chang. Or everyone named Smith in New York. You could spend the rest of your life and a few other lives sifting through them. This was what was wrong with the blacklist—an American unit seeking someone named, say, Nguyen Van Dong in a typical I Corps village would be confronted with possibly a dozen Nguyen Van Dongs. How to separate out the one on the blacklist? No way, unfortunately, because only the Nguyen Van Dong with the correct mark over the vowels in "Van" and "Dong" could distinguish the right person.

Thus the blacklist, assembled so patiently by interrogators, CI agents and U.S. units in the field, was as good as useless. All wasted. Only the lack of a language-trained observer like me had kept the error from being discovered before this, and only the presence of a language-trained observer could ensure that the error was never made again.

I strode into the office of Captain Roma, the CI commander, and without preamble said, "Captain, I hate to tell you this, but the blacklist isn't worth a damn." I then explained the reasoning behind my statement. Roma listened, fanning himself with a sheaf of agent reports. A pained expression grew on his otherwise pleasant face.

"Lieutenant Smith, I don't want to hear any more about this."

"Why not sir? Something has to be done. Maybe we can borrow some ARVN typewriters to get the names right from now on."

"Look, I'm going home in a couple of months. Everything has been going fine so far. We collect names, file them in neat little folders, and pass the information down to Saigon. Everybody is happy, period. Don't rock the boat, OK?"

Now my face took on a pained expression. "But sir . . ."

"Forget it, Smith! I'm not going to be the one to tell Saigon that its blacklist system is totally fucked up. Now just go back to what you were doing, and let's pretend you never even came in here. Dismissed."

And that was that. So much for using my language skills to help fight the war. This was my first serious encounter with army intransigence and inertia. It would be far from my last.

As I walked away form Roma's office with its neat little file folders, I regretted once again that I hadn't accepted Rob Sullivan's offer back at Fort Holabird. It was the last day of MI basic school, a crisp, almost painfully bright October day. Rob and I, who had struck up a friendship during our month there, had gone to Holabird's rather seedy officers club for a final lunch. Unlike all the other student-lieutenants, he had never talked about his next assignment. Over greasy but delicious cheeseburgers, he revealed in a low voice that he had been picked for the MI Office of Personnel Operations in Washington.

"OPO? My god, Rob, that means you get to assign MI officers all over the world. No wonder you were afraid to tell anyone here. They'd all be sucking up to you to get out of going to Vietnam. Come to think of it, this also means *you* don't have to go to Vietnam, you lucky son of a bitch."

"That's right, Eric. I think I was selected because I'm older than the rest of you guys. Anyway, since you and I got to be friends before you knew about OPO, I know we're really friends. And I take care of my buddies. Now, where do you want to go instead of Vietnam?"

The burger grease clotted in my throat. He was offering me a way out of Vietnam. By that time I already had orders to Vietnamese language school in El Paso, and it didn't take a brain surgeon to figure out that Vietnam itself was my next duty station after that. Now I was getting a second chance—the kind of opportunity to pick my own assignment that only well-connected senior officers got—and all because I had a friend in OPO. Where did I want to go, what exotic, cushy locale where I could fulfill my secret fantasy of being an ascot-wearing secret agent? Turkey? Rome? NATO headquarters in Brussels?

Instead, I said, "Thanks a lot, Rob, really, but I think I'll stick with what I've got." As tempted as I was, I could not have lived with the guilt of using a personal connection to get out of Vietnam when so many others had to go. Maybe I was just stupid, who knows? Rob was of course appalled, but he accepted my decision. He checked with me one more time, months later, when I was married and finishing up at language school in the West Texas desert. "Last chance, Eric," he said over the phone, "I have your Vietnam orders sitting right here on my desk." I hadn't changed my mind, though, so I let him put the orders through.

Still, shuffling through the stifling heat, listening to the distant thump of artillery on enemy-held hills west of Chu Lai, and burning at my rejection at the hands of an army hack like Captain Roma, I wondered if I had made the right decision. I am still wondering.

I had my own chance to get someone out of Vietnam, too, but this time the offer was accepted with glee. Back at the Americal combat center, only a day or two after I had arrived in country, I happened to overhear a group of five Puerto Rican soldiers discussing a frightening problem. My high school and college Spanish was good enough at the time to understand everything they were saying to each other, but of course they had no idea that this Anglo lieutenant nearby was listening to, much less understanding, their words. Their problem was that they had somehow never learned to speak English. They had done basic training and advanced infantry training together in Puerto Rico, and had been shipped to Vietnam without the army ever finding out about their language disability. Now they were less than a week away from joining combat units out in the bush, and they were sharing with each other their fears that they would die, or cause someone else to be killed, because they couldn't understand English.

I went over to chat with them, and when they saw I was an officer and a Spanish speaker, they begged for help. "What can I do?" I said, "I'm only an FNG second lieutenant here. I have no clout." Nevertheless, I agreed to try to bring their plight to the attention of the combat center commander, whose whitewashed hootch I found after a search of the compound. The whole interview took less than five minutes. "Are you sure they're telling the truth?" he asked me. "Absolutely, sir. They couldn't have known that I spoke Spanish and understood what they were saying to each other. These guys would definitely be in deep shit out in the field."

"Fine," the colonel said. "Tell them to be at the Chu Lai airstrip at 0600 tomorrow. They're going back to Puerto Rico to finish out their tours. And thank you, Lieutenant, for bringing this to my attention. This is why we run everyone through the combat center, to weed out unfit soldiers and catch the army's mistakes."

When I told the five Puerto Rican soldiers, they fell on my neck and kissed me. They carried me a few yards on their shoulders. They bought me a big dinner at the PX. And the next morning, they flew away from Vietnam on the freedom bird, leaving me wishing that I only spoke Spanish so I could go home, too. By that time I was beginning to wonder why I had been so hasty in refusing Rob Sullivan's offer of rescue.

Cursing Captain Roma under my breath, I returned to my office to complete my interrogation report, bungled blacklist names and all. Once or twice through the rest of the afternoon, my mind wandered back to images of joyous Puerto Rican soldiers dancing in the sand, and cheeseburgers on a bright October day. I didn't know then that very soon I would be taking my first trips away from Chu Lai, and on one of them I would long for the scruffy but familiar IPW compound as if it were my home back in the World.

# CHAPTER 8

# Tickets to Ride

I was going a little stir crazy at Chu Lai. I needed a change of scenery. Each day, from 7:00 A.M. until long after dark, my nose was pressed to one piece of paper or another—document reports, interrogation reports, EEI lists, blacklists, intelligence summaries, rosters, letters, notes, and the hated spot reports known as "twixes." I say hated because these twixes (the name derives from the army initials, TWX, and I still don't know for sure what they stood for) functioned as a kind of early warning to MACV (Military Assistance Command, Vietnam) headquarters in Saigon that an important prisoner or enemy document had been received at the Americal Division MID. As the scapegoat officer to whom all unpleasant duties seemed to be assigned, I was required to make sure such information was twixed to Saigon as soon as possible, in the middle of the night if necessary. And far too often for my taste, it was necessary.

I would be sleeping in my bunk soundly, or at least as soundly as anyone could while machine guns, flares, and howitzers were being fired off on the bunker line all night, when some interrogator would show up at my hootch door with a copy of a just-completed report in his hand. Our men frequently extended daytime prisoner interviews late into the evening if the detainees' importance warranted it, and it took more time after that to write up the results. "Twix for Saigon, sir," he would call out, indicating that something the prisoner said was significant enough to alert higher authorities. Mandatory twix alerts were also demanded by MID regulations if the prisoner was of a certain rank or belonged to a targeted unit. When a document was involved, the man at my door would be one of our interpreters or a readout specialist from the ARVN MID. I would roll out of my bunk, throw on a pair of fatigues and boots (sometimes without socks—I presumed I was safe from having to pass inspection at those ungodly hours) and jump into one of the three cranky IPW jeeps parked in the compound. Then I'd race, at speeds illegal even for Vietnam, a few miles down the road to the tactical operations center (TOC) in the middle of the division administration complex. Sometimes I had to drive through heavy monsoon rain in the uncovered vehicles, and a few times I had to run the gauntlet of a VC rocket attack in progress to deliver twixes "downtown."

There I would try to find a desk and typewriter that wasn't being used and convert the facts on the interrogation report to the telegraphlike format we employed to talk electronically with Saigon. I would make five carbon copies of the twix, each of which I would deliver by hand later to various darkened offices around the complex, and then bring the original over to the hot line for transmission. As the twenty-four hour nerve center of the division, the TOC was equipped with many different kinds of communications devices, and a few of them were rigged with special electronic cloaks against enemy interception. Even the low-tech VC could occasionally be capable of listening in on American conversations with the right equipment. Not being part of the elint (electronic intelligence) arm of the MI branch, I was ignorant of the workings of hot-line devices, but I did at least know where to find the twix desk.

I would return to my bunk, often hours later, to complete my beauty sleep until the no-exceptions rising hour of 7:00 A.M. After more than a month of midnight interruptions, I was chronically tired, short-tempered, and prone to involuntary catnaps in the middle of the day. Still, it was better than going on night ambush patrols for the infantry. Or so I kept reminding myself.

So I was understandably eager for a change of pace. For some time, I had been thinking of making a visit to one of the three brigade IPW sections. It was part of my job to familiarize myself with all aspects of the American's informa-

tion collection process, but I was also interested in what
went on beyond the barbed-wire fences of the division base
camp. I was especially curious about those strutting, cool-
eyed lieutenants who commanded MI teams at our brigades.
These men were, in a manner of speaking, on the bottom of
the MI heap. They were at the lowest-level unit to which a
trained MI branch officer was assigned in Vietnam. They
were the only officers wearing our branch insignia (a brass
collar device depicting what we were told at Fort Holabird
was the "rose of secrecy" superimposed over a compass
symbol and a medieval broadsword—we nicknamed it "the
shafted pansy") at their base camps. Nevertheless, in my
mind these independent lieutenants represented unfettered
freedom of action and on-the-spot service to troops in the
field. James Bond in a helmet, if you will—and closer to
my college-boy image of intelligence operatives than the
pettifogging desk drivers I had seen at division headquarters.

I informed Captain Steele of my desire to go, and he
agreed it would be a fine idea for me to take an informal
inspection tour of a brigade outfit. Two days later, I
climbed aboard a UH-1 Huey helicopter at the chopper pad
beside the IPW compound and took off for Duc Pho, site
of the 11th Brigade base camp thirty miles south. It was my
first ride in that now-legendary aircraft, and a memorable
one mainly because it was the first time I'd been cool since
I arrived in country. Several thousand feet above the siz-
zling ground, the chilled, fast-moving air rushing through
the open doors was sheer ecstasy to my overheated body.
Out to the left I could see bare, yellow little islands bobbing in the deep blue South China Sea. Below, the coastal
beach ran to the hazy southern horizon line, and on my
right, mountains obscured the western horizon.

In a letter to my wife that night, after I returned, I described my experiences and thoughts:

> I used to think that real, practical intelligence was
> produced at division level, but I now know that the intel-
> ligence game is played for keeps down at brigade level.
> These guys get a dink into the cage, grill him, and if he
> knows where a base camp or a rice cache or a [VC]

meeting is—the brigade IPW people get a chopper, a platoon or two and bring the dink right back to where it is. . . . It is a system of immediate reward—the intelligence officer at brigade level can actually see how his information is used and how accurate it is. We at division do warmed-over . . . reports for the files.

My counterpart at the 11th took me all around the cage, the document section, the interrogation section, everywhere. He introduced me to everyone and let me go through all of their files on local VC units, which helped me immensely to understand what they faced down there. Then he took me down to the little village of Duc Pho, which looks like our own An Tan [the village outside the American base camp], except dirtier. He is known down there, and we were invited to share *nuoc tra* (sweet boiled tea) with several families. The inside of these hootches is even dirtier, smaller and [more] fly-ridden than the outsides, but the Vietnamese are basically clean and do the best they can with wooden sides, tin roofs and dirt floors.

Everywhere you go in Duc Pho there are signs of the VC. Bunkers, bridges and churches were all destroyed by local VC sapper units [probably during the Tet Offensive seven months before]. . . . If I were sent out to a brigade, I wouldn't gripe too much, although I'd never volunteer to go.

That's what I told my wife, anyway. She would have worried if I sounded too enthusiastic about this initial glimpse of another, more exciting—and ultimately more dangerous—way to practice the intelligence craft in Vietnam. But I was more than simply enthusiastic. As I flew back to Chu Lai in a C-123 cargo plane, I reviewed my disturbingly mixed feelings. I knew that a chance might come during my time at the Americal to command one of the division's three brigade intelligence units. I might even be granted the opportunity to decline it or accept it. If I said yes, I would get first dibs on prisoner and document information and then see it used by the infantry almost immediately. I had seen that much during my visit to Duc Pho, and

I loved the idea of using my MI and language training so directly.

A brigade assignment, on the other hand, was the opposite of a safe assignment. Compared to sprawling, well-protected division installations like Chu Lai, the smaller brigade base camps were more exposed to enemy ground assaults and attacks by rockets and mortar fire. Brigade intelligence personnel worked a lot more closely with the infantry, exposing themselves, again, to getting shot. If I got to command a brigade team, I would be on my own most of the time, far away from my nearest superior officer, and far away, too, from the protective, comforting presence of the big Chu Lai complex. I wanted a brigade slot, and at the same time I was scared to death of getting one. Later experience would teach me that I was both right and wrong to feel this way.

Back at Chu Lai I gave a verbal report of my trip to Captain Steele and resumed my normal duties. The incident of the blacklist continued to bother me, but today I realize that my youth and inexperience were working against me then. Now, with the benefit of two decades of hindsight, I would handle the situation differently. So what if Captain Roma was afraid of rocking the blacklist boat? I could have gone over his head to less rigid and fearful authorities and made a vigorous case for correcting such an outrageous flaw in the system. If the MID commander or senior staff officers at the Americal were still unwilling to take action, I could have gone beyond them by making a report directly to the 525th Military Intelligence Group in Saigon or even MACV headquarters itself. If this was insubordination then so be it. Defective blacklists were too important to be ignored, and today I know that the proper authorities would have been glad to know how to improve them from someone who had been trained to do just that. Besides, what could the big brass do to me for pressing my case too forcefully—send me to Vietnam?

I continued to watch interrogations others were doing, but by this time I also felt comfortable facing prisoners with only an interpreter for company. At no point did I ever believe that my language ability was advanced enough to conduct an interrogation alone, although it was more than adequate to keep general tabs on what my interpreter was asking and hearing back. There would be no *Mot, hai, ba, buon, nam, shau, bay, tam, chin, muoi* incidents for me, or at least none that I knew of. The prisoners themselves were surprisingly docile. They seldom, if ever, showed outright resistance to questioning and most of the time behaved as if they were under mild sedation. Perhaps the shock of being captured silenced them, or maybe their culture predisposed them to accept whatever happened without protest. I was never sure, but just in case all interrogators were told to leave their weapons outside the cage. I witnessed no escape attempts while I was at division, and I only heard of two incidents that had occurred before I arrived, when prisoners tried to get away. In both cases they never made it more than a few yards from the PW cage before recapture by the MPs. I was of course relieved that prisoners posed no threat to my safety, but after a while I did notice that my attitude toward them became increasingly callous. This, I felt, could be dangerous. It would be all too easy to start mistreating passive, obedient prisoners and maybe even torturing them. As time went on, I had to struggle to keep the sadistic urges inside me under rigid control, and much later on I would have to watch for signs of this in my men. On a couple of occasions, which I will talk about in a future chapter, these urges went temporarily out of control.

Every time I sat down to a typewriter to fill out an interrogation report, I remembered old Sergeant Blineberry back at Georgetown ROTC and his everlasting hatred of army chickenshit. My own burden of chickenshit was Captain Steele's dictum that all interrogation reports be perfectly typed. Perfectly. No margin for error. If, in the process of producing a five- or ten-page report, I misspelled a word or struck over a typo or reversed a number sequence, I would have to remove the offending page and type it all over again—and again—until it was right. I was not allowed to make corrections of any kind with a pen, which, God and the army forbid, would have been a lot easier and faster. To make matters worse, each report had to be typed on five additional carbons because in Chu Lai in those days there were no Xerox or IBM copy machines for us to use. Somewhere down in the bureaucratic bowels of MACV in Saigon there existed such miracle machines, but we in the boondocks wouldn't see them any time soon. To correct one error, therefore, I was required to remove the original page and its five carbonized brothers from my typewriter and start all over again. This was the kind of lint-picking I expected to find inside the E-ring at the Pentagon, not in a wooden hootch in the middle of a combat zone. We were at war, after all, and a little sloppiness might be forgiven. But not by Captain Steele, whose fastidiousness in the matter of paperwork would earn him my undying animosity and whose stiff-necked attitude caused countless delays in the flow of information to those who wanted it, typos notwithstanding.

My second trip away from Chu Lai was anything but voluntary. After dinner on the evening of August 27, I was relaxing in my hootch by writing a long letter to my wife. To remind myself that I was still a civilian soldier, I wore a pair of old gray flannel slacks and an Izod shirt I had packed into my overseas kit back in Knoxville. The pants were torn along the right thigh where I had hooked them on a protruding nail on my way out the door at fifty mph during a recent rocket attack. Captain Steele walked in, glancing disdainfully at my civvies, and said, "Get into your combat gear, Smith, you're going for a chopper ride."

"Where to, sir?" I tried to keep my voice steady, as if I were long accustomed to flying away into the night on combat missions.

"We've got a big contact (battle) going with the 1st VC Regiment up on Cigar Island. Somebody there reported uncovering a cache of important enemy documents. They're supposed to be written in Chinese. I want you to go up and bring them back for an immediate readout."

"How do I get my hands on a chopper, Captain?"

"I already did it for you. Be at the IPW pad in twenty minutes. Take your weapon."

# CHAPTER 9

# Mother's Pride

I waited by the edge of the cracked blacktop of the helicopter pad, hurriedly checking over my equipment. My chopper should be arriving any minute.

This would be the first time I needed to wear full combat gear. My helmet, even with a liner inside, was too big for my small head. It wobbled when I walked, making me look like a mushroom in motion. The flak vest was inflexible and heavy. My web gear included a first-aid–bandage pouch, canteen (which I had forgotten to fill), two large ammunition pouches, and holstered .45 pistol with ammo magazines. I also carried a World War II vintage .30-caliber M-1 carbine, a weapon I had purchased for forty dollars from one of the interpreters. This choice of weapon was a little unorthodox, but I had put a lot of thought into it.

My rifle training back in the states had been first with the venerable M-1 Garand and later with its beefed-up version, the M-14 assault rifle. Only at the very end, on a desert firing range outside El Paso, did I receive any instruction at all in the army's new M-16 rifle, and that wasn't much. I liked the M-16 well enough; it was lighter by three pounds than either of its predecessors; it carried more rounds in its box magazine and was fitted with a switch for full automatic fire. Shooting it was as light and easy as squirting a garden hose. But I hadn't been taught to fieldstrip it under pressure. I hadn't learned how to unjam it in an emergency. I hadn't carried it around for days in all kinds of weather. I hadn't slept with it next to me in a tent.

In short, I hadn't "familiarized" myself with that rifle, or at least not enough to trust my life to it.

So, when I got to Vietnam and was issued a brand new M-16, I promptly placed it my wall locker and went looking for something else to carry. Since I had developed a great affection for the simple, rugged, dependable old M-1 Garand, I figured I would obtain one somewhere. No luck. U.S. and ARVN troops had long since adopted fancier, more advanced firearms. The little brother of the M-1, the M-1 carbine, was still around in large numbers, however, probably because the Vietnamese soldier, who was generally short, preferred its reduced size, weight, and recoil. Ammo for the carbine, the low-powered .30-caliber round, was also plentiful. So I happily paid a black-market premium to one of the IPW interpreters who just happened to have a carbine for sale.

It was indeed a short, light weapon and pleasant to fire in practice. I remembered too late, however, that I had never received any training on this somewhat obsolete weapon, either, and thus was completely ignorant of its inner workings and quirks. Its mechanical similarity to the M-1 Garand was in fact slight, but I carried it anyway, hoping I'd never have to use it in combat. Fat chance.

I was going on this trip without an interpreter because my mission was simply to retrieve the "Chinese" documents and get back to Chu Lai as fast as I could. Due to the uncertain situation, my return travel arrangements were, well, vague. The Americal's only tank squadron, the 1/1 Cavalry, was at that moment engaged in the biggest battle I would witness while I was in Vietnam. It was taking place on a wide barrier beach we called Cigar Island that lay just off the South China Sea coast north of Chu Lai. The 1st Main Force VC Regiment had apparently been massing for an attack on the nearby provincial capital city of Tam Ky when our tank force bumped into it, probably by accident. Between August 24 and 29, the two forces fought a loosely structured, running battle whose boundaries spread up, down, and across Cigar Island. The sandy marshlands were better suited to tank warfare than triple-canopy jungle, which is why the 1/1 Cav was based there in the first place. For their part, the VC fought small-unit engagements whenever possible and sniped constantly at our troops from tree lines and spider holes dug into the ground. It was a frustrating, nasty battle that eventually produced high casualties on both sides.

Even as I scrambled into the Huey helicopter taking me to the temporary field headquarters of the 1/1 Cav, I knew my mission was completely useless. I had tried to tell Captain Steele before I left that the "Chinese" documents were in all likelihood prayer scrolls routinely deposited in Vietnamese graves. The ancient language of Vietnam, before the influence of French teachers and priests, was written in Chinese characters. Traditional prayers, stroked with brush and ink on long rolls of rice paper, were still inscribed that way and placed in graves at the time of burial. I had seen many of these militarily irrelevant documents come across my documents desk. Some American tank had probably churned up a graveyard with its treads and popped out a few stray burial scrolls. But Captain Steele, as usual, dismissed my opinion and insisted I risk my ass on a futile run up to embattled Cigar Island.

I must admit that the trip was exhilarating. Once again I was cool, sliding through the evening air, high above villages and silvery rivers. Out on the darkening sea, I could see little Cu Lao Re Island, where rumor had it that an old guerrilla holdout (from the days when the Viet Minh fought against France) allegedly took a shot at every passing ship and plane. A mile or two to the west, a flight of F-4 Phantom jets was bombing and strafing a smoke-wreathed hamlet to rubble. I spotted the 1/1 Cav encampment as we descended to a cleared patch of Cigar Island; it was a cluster of jeeps, two-and-a-half-ton trucks, tents, and conexes, prefabricated metal containers that resembled room-size trash dumpsters. From the air it looked like a western wagon train pulled in a circle against the Indians, and in a way it was.

The chopper dropped onto the landing zone. I waved to the pilot (my last link with safety as far as I was concerned), jumped out, and trotted about fifty yards over to the ring of vehicles and conexes. In the distance I could hear artillery and small-arms fire. Flashes of light streaked the sky. The battle seemed to be uncomfortably close. Asking around inside the main structure, an oversize conex crowded with communications gear and scurrying clerks, I was finally introduced to the grimy, unshaven tanker who had brought in the documents. As soon as he pulled them out of his unbuttoned fatigue shirt, I knew they were duds—burial scrolls inscribed with prayers in Chinese characters. "My tank dug these up today," he said. Just as I thought. Just as I had told Captain Steele. Red China certainly wasn't entering the war, and I was stuck with a smelly wad of rice paper.

I hid this downbeat conclusion from the tanker and thanked him. He had done the right thing, after all. Then I asked one of the commo clerks for a radio link to Chu Lai so I could make my report to Captain Steele. I faced a bit of a dilemma here; if I revealed the uselessness of the documents I had come for, Captain Steele would be tempted to let me stay up there with the Cav until the battle had subsided or a regularly scheduled logistical helicopter could be dispatched to pick me up. Why not let that know-it-all Smith stew in a conex for a while? That could take a couple of days or more. If, on the other hand, I simply held my tongue, gave no opinion of the documents' importance and requested an immediate pickup, Steele would use his intelligence clout to rustle up a helicopter for me within an hour or two. I had already noticed the steady stream of medevac (medical evacuation) choppers flying overhead. It was obvious we were taking a lot of casualties, and all available choppers had been assigned to the Cav battle zone. Those aircraft were full of wounded and dying soldiers, and if one of them had to be diverted to retrieve me, lives or limbs could be lost in the process. It was not a happy choice.

I decided to waffle. Maybe Steele could find a nonmedevac chopper to get me? Maybe I was wrong about the burial documents? I really wanted to get back home to Chu Lai because I had a feeling the battle zone was drifting closer, and I had no place being there. Small-arms fire was increasing in intensity just over the hill. Shells seemed to be bursting nearby. My instinct that something was wrong wasn't wrong. Later I found out that the infantry company normally assigned to guard the headquarters complex had been drawn into the fighting. In fact no one was defending this wagon train circle of clerks and armchair officers. And elements of the 1st VC Regiment were infiltrating into the area even as I spoke with Captain Steele over the crackling airwaves.

"Sir, what do you want me to do? Over."

"Smith, what's your take on those documents? Are they written in Chinese or not? Over."

"Yes sir, they are. Over." I was telling the truth, after all, answering a direct question with a direct, if incomplete, answer.

"Okay, I'm going to get a medevac chopper to drop down and pick you up. It should be there in about an hour. Watch for the landing lights, but it won't come down all the way. It will hover a few feet up; you climb on and tell the pilot to bring you back to the IPW pad. Out."

And that was that. I was going to get a fast ride home. Maybe the medevac chopper would be empty; maybe not. I felt guilty but immensely relieved.

I waited, positioning myself by the conex exit that faced the chopper pad. Night fell completely, and the battle noises rolled closer. Reports from units in contact with VC forces came in over the radios. The voices sounded nervous, even alarmed. The clerks and radio operators became edgy.

I thought I saw a black spot appear on one of the conex walls. Then another. They weren't spots—they were holes, holes being punctured through the metal skin. "We're taking fire!" someone yelled. "Incoming!" Clerks leaped back from their tables, clustering in the center of the conex. Some of them dropped to the floor. Officers appeared, shouting for men to grab their weapons. They told others to start destroying radio codebooks. Soldiers swirled around the complex in confusion. The faint but pungent odor of panic sweat was in the air.

It wasn't clear exactly what was happening. Some rifle bullets may have penetrated the walls, true, but the firing wasn't steady, and it could have come from our own troops nearby. "Friendly fire" had been known to wound and kill U.S. troops before, especially in the confusion of combat. Or it could have been flying shrapnel from bursting shells. Then I saw a larger hole appear, although no explosion followed. The VC we faced were armed with a number of heavy weapons—RPG rocket launchers, Chinese-made 57mm recoilless rifles, 8mm mortars, antitank rifles—the hole could have been made by any one of them.

Some officers present thought we were under attack, however, and they gave orders accordingly. Small fires sprang up inside the conex where clerks had set them to burn documents and code manuals. Someone outside was returning fire. Radios were smashed with rifle butts. Thick, oily smoke from known and unknown sources spread through the conex I was standing in. A sort of controlled chaos broke out. I felt for my carbine, opened the flap of my .45 holster. The rice-paper scrolls were tucked inside my fatigue shirt; I hoped for the chopper to come for me soon.

Then I heard the beat of blades in the darkness outside. A chopper had detached itself from the line of aircraft overhead and was circling down to the Cav pad. Slowly, uncertainly, feeling its way through the light-streaked sky.

This must be my ride. Oh, goody.

A figure materialized a few feet away, out of the billows of smoke obscuring the interior of the conex. It was the assistant division commander, a fat, rosy-faced brigadier general, who must have been there to honcho the battle from the Cav's impromptu headquarters. He calmly carried a cocked .45 in one hand, and with the other he reached out to my shoulder. Gripping the area around my collarbone with his chubby paw, this general said to me over the din of shouting clerks and machine-gun fire, "Son, your mother would be proud of you today!"

I guess he was trying to rally the troops, or at least the one young lieutenant he spied in the confusion. I hardly knew what to reply—in any case, my transportation was down to a few feet of altitude over the pad fifty yards away. It was time to go. "Sir, fuck you, sir!" I howled at him as I stepped outside and sprinted to the waiting chopper.

I don't know what made me say that. I had no personal beef with the general and wished him well with his old-fashioned but, as far as I could see, totally ineffective effort to comfort the panicking clerks back there. Maybe I was just getting tired of army chickenshit. Under the circumstances, old Sergeant Blineberry at Georgetown might have understood my disrespect to a superior officer. The superior officer, though, had absolutely no goddam idea who I was, and for that I was grateful.

With my arms coiled around the chopper's cold landing skids, I shot into the night sky moaning and mumbling the Lord's Prayer in sheer fright. I didn't dare look down. After what seemed like thousands of feet of altitude later, a crewman hauled me into the wildly tilting helicopter and unceremoniously dumped me onto the steel floorplates. I have no doubt he was angry at being ordered to postpone the return trip to Chu Lai in order to retrieve some intelligence geek. Only red running lights illuminated the inside of the Huey. I felt something sticky under my hands. A jumble of bodies, some living and some dead, lay on the deck around me. We all pitched and tossed together in the rhythm with the chopper's erratic movements.

"Jesus, Smitty, is that you?" one of the bodies said.

Crawling closer to it and peering through the eerie glare, I recognized the face of Warren Witzener, a lieutenant I had known back at the Americal combat center. His right arm was heavily bandaged, and his uniform was slathered in blood.

Warren and I had been part of an informal "club" of five lieutenants who ate meals together and kibitzed around with each other whenever possible during the week we were at the center. We had been, with one exception, new second lieutenants with no idea of what we would be facing when we got to our respective units, so we wasted a lot of pleasant time together speculating about our upcoming tours. The exception was a slightly older first lieutenant named Phil Talbott, a National Guard officer who had been called up for duty in Vietnam. In private we often referred to him as "that poor son of a bitch Talbott" because our impression was that National Guardsmen became National Guardsmen to avoid duty in Vietnam, not to end up serving there. He was either an unlucky one or, if he had volunteered, a stupid one.

By far the oddest member of the group was Mike Pojeski. He started talking from the first moment he sat at the combat center mess hall table with us (uninvited) until the last second of the last evening at the center. His rapid-fire, one-way conversation was a bizarre mix of complaints, exhortations, declarations, threats, and incoherent rambling. His politics appeared to be right-wing, but on other days they appeared to be doctrinaire Communist. I could never sort it all out. To me it was a wonder this young man ever stayed out of a mental institution, but by some quirk of the system he not only made it through college ROTC but actually earned a commission. We all tolerated his unexplained outbursts and constant lectures on everything from military history to the sexual customs of the girls in his Oregon hometown, but we feared for the lives of the men the man would be commanding within a matter of days.

The last member of the group was an infantry branch officer we nicknamed "the Indian" because he was one-half Cherokee. He was taciturn to the point of dead silence, but for some reason he sought out our company, and we allowed him to.

I bring up this "club" because I would see or hear of each one before I left Vietnam and learn how their tours turned out. They would pop up in my life at odd moments throughout the months, usually in some dramatic way, and with very different stories to tell. We were a randomly assorted bunch who just happened to process through the American combat center at the same time and who happened to band together for a brief period. What happened to us in Vietnam may or may not have been typical of others' experience, but I will say now that, except for me, this was generally a hellishly, ill-starred group.

Warren was the first one I encountered, only weeks after leaving the combat center, and I could see his tour was about to end abruptly. After we parted he had been assigned to the 1/1 Cavalry as an armor platoon commander. Earlier that day, he told me over the din of whirling helicopter blades and groaning men, shouting men, he had been out on Cigar Island riding atop one of his tanks.

"We saw some dinks shooting at us from a tree line up ahead," he said, "so I waved to the tanks behind me to follow my lead. We were going to just run over those dinks with our treads, like we had been doing all day, you know.

"Well, when I waved my arm, this dink suddenly pops

out of a spider hole right in front of the tank and lets go with a rocket from his RPG. The fuckin' thing didn't fly far enough to go off (fuses for antitank rockets were set to detonate only after a certain distance), but it went right through my arm. Took it off at the elbow." He pointed to what was clearly a stump under the bandages.

"It's funny, you know. I brought my arm forward to wave the guys on, and then I saw my arm lying on the deck of my tank. It was weird."

I could tell Warren was still in shock. He alternated between giving me a straightforward account of the battle and asking me over and over again if I had any Scotch for him to drink. "Remember those good old days at the combat center?" he said once. Since I had neglected to fill my own canteen, I found one on the floor and let him drink from it. I told him I had to deliver some documents, but I would be back up to the evacuation hospital to visit him later that night.

The chopper finally came to rest at the IPW pad long enough for me to roll out. My fatigues were wet with Warren's blood. Captain Steele and I had a brief conference, during which I did the best I could not to say "I told you so" and failed. He wanted the rice-paper scrolls translated anyway, so I gave them to our best interpreter, Sergeant Minh, and told him to do his best. Minh looked confused. Being a modern Vietnamese, he didn't speak, write, or understand a word of Chinese. I knew this, and suggested that he write up an important-looking report in which he declared, after much creative bullshitting, that these scrolls were in fact burial documents of no intelligence value. Then I grabbed a jeep and drove to the hospital.

The 312th Evacuation Hospital sat on a cliff above the South China Sea at the edge of our headquarters complex. It was a beautiful location for a very unpleasant place. This was where all American and Vietnamese (including the enemy) casualties were taken directly after being wounded in the field. Dead bodies were flown there, too. I found Warren in the intensive care unit, now clean and relatively comfortable on a cot. I asked if he wanted to get word to his parents back in Wisconsin that he had lost his arm. He said no.

"Don't you want to prepare them for when you come home, Warren? The army might have already notified them that you were wounded in action."

"I'm not ready to tell them about my arm," he said. His eyes were full of tears.

It took me a while, but at last I convinced him it was better to let his parents know now than to shock them into fainting on the spot when he walked off the plane in Wisconsin with a stump instead of a right arm. He couldn't write, of course, so I took down what he wanted to say and gave it to the Red Cross representative at the hospital to send out that night.

"You're lucky in a way, Warren," I said, "you're going home alive. You're going home early, and with a Purple Heart. The army will get you a prosthetic arm and you'll be almost as good as new. Don't worry, okay?" But he was asleep by then, clutching an empty cup of water in his good left hand. I wondered if *his* mother would be proud of him.

I walked out of the hospital, trying not to look at the wounded and dying men lying everywhere. Unfortunately, I would be back there very soon.

# CHAPTER 10

# Whitemare

Captain Rufus Steele was a punctilious man. He believed not only in doing everything by the book, but in doing everything by footnotes in the book. Thus if the manual of MI security procedures decreed that all filing cabinets must be locked up when the office was empty, then by God that would be done under any and all circumstances, no matter what. Come hell or high water.

Hell happened rather suddenly one afternoon shortly after my trip to the 1/1 Cav when, contrary to normal practice, the neighboring VC decided to lob rockets into our base camp in broad daylight. About high noon, in fact. Just in time to ruin lunch. These rocket attacks weren't necessarily directed at the IPW compound. Indeed, if the VC had any sense they'd try to avoid killing their own people held inside the prisoner of war cage. But our compound lay just to the east of the Chu Lai airfield, and we figured that, given the assuredly low level of rocketry training among the malarial peasants who made up local VC forces, the 122mm and 140mm rockets that plowed into our compound out of the western mountains were most probably accidental overshoots. Those flying garbage cans the VC and NVA used for rockets weren't exactly designed for pinpoint accuracy, anyway, so IPW got rockets that were clearly intended for a militarily more significant target, the airfield.

But even a rocket aimed at someone else can do damage if it lands near you. When I heard the first explosions from inside the office, like the other occupants I bolted for the door in a frenzied race to the nearest bunker. It was almost a luxury to be able to find my way in the sunlight, because I was so used to scurrying around in the dark during the normal nighttime attacks.

"Hold it, Lieutenant Smith! Where are you going?"

I stopped with my hand pressed against the screen door. Was that Captain Steele's voice I heard? "Uh, sir, I was going to the bunker."

"Not until we lock up. Give me a hand here."

I could hardly believe it. Steele was actually going to secure the pathetic little clumps of classified documents we had lying around the office. He was determined to go by the book, by golly, even in the midst of a rain of rockets. Who knows—maybe an intrepid (or terminally stupid) enemy agent, who just happened to be lurking around, was going to sneak in and purloin some low-level reports or pencil-requisition forms? I traced my steps back into the office with what I believed was understandable reluctance. Huge, booming explosions were unfolding themselves outside, and shrapnel was lacerating the air. Everyone else had departed for bunkerland. Everyone sane, that is.

I ran around the office scooping up whatever documents looked important and tossed them into an open file cabinet, trying not to look terrified. Steele methodically gathered papers and placed them in their proper file folders. Ten minutes later, when the job was completed to his satisfaction, Steele slid the file drawers closed, ran a steel bar through eyelets bolted to the drawers, and fixed a government-issue padlock to a ring at the top of the bar. The finishing touch was a little red metal flag inserted in the top drawer handle to indicate that the cabinet contents were secure—all exactly according to Hoyle and the holy MI manual.

But it was too late. The air was silent, the attack was over. The "all clear" sounded on the division's chronically tardy air raid siren, and men began to filter back into the office from their respective bunkers. Without a word, Captain Steele unlocked the file cabinet and handed folders to the passing men for redistribution around their desks.

As I say, this was a finicky fellow.

"Smith, we need someone over at the hospital to do interrogations, and you're it," Steele said to me in his office the next morning. His fine sense of order was offended by the fact that VC and NVA soldiers wounded in the field were flown directly to the 312th Evacuation Hospital at Chu Lai without being questioned. There they were treated and shipped out to other locations through medical channels. If anyone ever got around to interrogating these wounded prisoners later, none of us at division IPW ever heard of it. This could be a big leak in the prisoner of war processing system that Steele was so dedicated to administering.

In fairness to Steele, I must say he was dead right. A wounded Vietnamese male, especially one of military age, meant he had been somewhere he probably wasn't supposed to be, i.e., in the line of fire. That didn't necessarily make him a confirmed enemy soldier, but a gunshot or shrapnel wound was at least arguable evidence that he had been shooting at Americans or in a location where a firefight was taking place. A suspicious battle wound was one possible way of sorting out enemy soldiers from the mass of "neutral" civilians.

At this point I should explain a little more about the rough-and-ready system we used to designate classes of prisoners. Innocent civilians (ICs) were just that—ordinary, law-abiding Vietnamese who wouldn't hurt a fly and who certainly never harbored nasty thoughts about their American allies. An IC was often a person who had been abruptly seized for no apparent reason by American troops in one of their random village roundups. ICs, who were usually women, old men, or children, came in without capture tags or with nonincriminating information on their capture tags. After a quick screening, generally at the brigade level, they were released.

Prisoners of war (POWs) were men, and sometimes women, whose interrogations showed that they were VC or NVA soldiers. These would be questioned at the brigade and division levels before being shipped off to a corps collection point and ultimately a permanent prison camp. POWs with special information to impart or high rank were sent to the Combined Military Interrogation Center in Saigon, where my buddies from language school and other experts would debrief them in detail.

The most troublesome category was the one called civil

defendant (CD). These were supposed to be people who had violated the laws of South Vietnam, but who were not proven enemy soldiers. What you might call a catchall classification. Because none of us in IPW had studied, or even looked at, any laws of South Vietnam at any time, however, we hadn't the faintest idea of whether an individual had violated one of them or not. Somewhere in the office filing cabinets that Captain Steele so zealously guarded there was probably a memo outlining the basic legal code of the South Vietnamese government, yet I don't remember ever reading one or having one brought to my attention.

To classify a detainee as a CD, therefore, I learned to do what every other uninformed interrogator did, namely to use a crude rule of thumb: if the detainee had been caught shooting at an American, or harboring an enemy soldier, or keeping an arms cache, or belonging to a Communist association (did the VC have Communist Lions Clubs? Communist Optimist Clubs?), then I assumed that some South Vietnamese law somewhere prohibited these unfriendly activities and classified the unlucky detainee as a CD.

The other problem with CDs was their disposition. They couldn't be released, and they didn't merit prison camp, so where could we send them? Our cooperative allies, the ARVNs, took care of that in their typically messy fashion. After questioning, CDs were trucked to the nearest ARVN detention camp for CDs. Thus they left American jurisdiction and became an ARVN problem. I never saw one of these facilities, and I never learned exactly where they were in relation to the American base camp, but I did hear plenty of rumors. Some stories said that CDs were released after paying a bribe to their guards. Other stories said that all CDs were mistreated horribly and finally dumped in semiofficial prison camps. No two rumors were alike.

The real fault in this system was that completely unqualified American interrogators were given the legally questionable power to play both judge and jury for Vietnamese civilians who might or might not have broken any laws, and who might or ight not have been imprisoned as a result. Still, that was the only system we had, so we used it, despite personal misgivings.

As the IPW section chief, Captain Steele was concerned

that bonafide enemy soldiers and VC guerrillas were slipping through the net over at the hospital. Sure, some ICs were being wounded out in the hamlets and rice paddies by trigger-happy U.S. troops, stray artillery rounds, and misguided aircraft attacks. It was far more likely, though, based on the fact that they were hurt in action, that many POWs and at least a few CDs were escaping interrogation simply because they needed medical attention. Steele intended to close the net with me.

To my knowledge, no MI officer had been assigned to hospital interrogation duty before, so I would get to invent the rules and then write the book for whoever followed me. It would not be an easy or edifying book, as I found out from day one.

After checking in with the hospital authorities to let them know why I was there, I stationed myself at the emergency room door. This, I presumed correctly, was where all incoming wounded would be delivered. I had no idea what to expect when the first medevac choppers flopped onto the pad outside and disgorged their grisly cargoes.

The double doors flew open and a flurry of activity, only a little of which I understood, followed. Doctors and nurses (the only round-eyed women I would ever see in Vietnam) directed the stretcher-bearers with their burdens to locations around the concrete floor of the ER. A line of green canvas stretchers came through, each with a wounded Vietnamese or American lying on it. The medical staff made no distinctions between friend and foe; as far as I could see everyone received the same lifesaving attention from the obviously dedicated healers. The noise sounded like the sound track of a horror film: beating chopper blades; shouting, crying, groaning men; doctors and nurses yelling above the din; the crash of the surf below.

I was standing close to the doors when a Vietnamese man loosely swathed in body bandages swept through on his stretcher. His left arm dangled oddly out of the wrappings and brushed against me as he went past. The arm fell off, thumping onto the floor. Someone retrieved it immediately, but I found myself gaping and gasping in shock. More wounded poured in—men waving bloody stumps in pain, men without feet, men with steaming holes in their torsos, men whose heads were missing clumps of hair and skull.

The floor got slimy, then became awash in gore. Human parts and bright crimson bandages and fluids sluiced together, welling up until I could no longer see the bottoms of my boots. Men screamed and begged for their mothers without restraint or embarrassment. It was the most monstrously sickening scene I had ever beheld or ever would. It was Dante's Inferno at the seventh, abysmal level of descent. A waking nightmare in white.

I backed up to a gurney and fell against it. I could feel my eyes peeling up into the tops of my lids as my head rolled. My breath wouldn't come. I think I fainted for a few seconds. Dropping my clipboard, I lurched through the doors, stumbled over to a tiny bush growing a few feet beyond the carnage, and threw my guts up. I knew the bush lived through it, because months later I found one of the men who was replacing me at the hospital vomiting onto the same bush after his first hour in the ER. Somehow it had even grown a bit bigger.

Nobody told me it would be like that, but I still had work to do in there. Recovering my composure along with my clipboard, I searched through the rows of stretchers for a likely-looking VC or NVA suspect. Belatedly, I remembered I had an interpreter with me, an ARVN sergeant named Duc, who had apparently seen enough death over his service time that he was unmoved by viewing it again. I spotted a military-age Vietnamese male being transferred to a gurney and followed him. He was not too badly wounded—a real drawing card for me in those first shocking hours. The man was being wheeled over to an X-ray machine, and he looked scared to death of it.

Reasoning that he had never encountered such a device before and had no idea of its purpose, I quickly stood over him and said the first wild thing that came to my head.

"This machine is going to sterilize you," I told him through my interpreter. "You will never be able to have babies. But I can change the settings on the machine to avoid harming you if you tell me what you were doing when you were wounded."

He stared up at me in stark fear. "I was shooting at the Americans," he said in a low voice.

Bingo! My first patient, my first bold-faced lie (as well as my first attack of vomiting), and already I had a probable VC. "Are you VC?" I asked, moving my hand toward a dial on the X-ray machine. The technician looked coldly at me, but didn't interfere.

"Yes. I belong to my village self-defense force."

I began writing down his answers and in no time had enough information for a report. I then told the trembling VC trooper that, at my command, the machine would only examine his insides for bullet damage. He could have as many babies as he could sire. To this day I tremble myself whenever I have to get under an X-ray machine. It's a left-over guilt reaction for having to frighten all those poor bastards I interrogated at the 312th Evac X-ray station. I deserve it.

After an hour or two in the ER, during which time three loads of wounded came in, I dismissed Sergeant Duc and went outside for a cigarette. The air smelled blessedly free of burned flesh, medicine, and cleaning solvent. I watched a pair of chaplains, one Protestant and the other Roman Catholic, chatting together by one of the ward entrances. On impulse, I walked over and asked the Catholic priest if we could talk for a moment. He was wearing captain's bars on his collar, but I addressed him out of habit as "father." I explained that I was raised Roman Catholic, and that I was having a hell of a time resolving the conflict between my duty as an intelligence officer and my religious upbringing, which in general terms taught me not to lie and be nasty to sick people.

His answer was quick in coming. "You're an American soldier, and these are dinks who've been killing people. Do your duty, Lieutenant."

"Thank you, Captain" (I now called him by his rank, which clearly outranked his status as priest in his mind). I saluted and walked away, never again to make the mistake of asking a military man, even one disguised as a holy man, for moral guidance.

The next day, and for the next few months, I went back to the hospital to do my job. I learned quickly to wear dark glasses and keep my eyes squinted almost shut behind them so I wouldn't see anything too clearly. With my clipboard and interpreter, I prowled the ER, the ICU (intensive care unit) and the wards for suspected enemy soldiers lying on cots, wrapped in bloody bandages, and hooked to rubber tubes. The medical staff treated me like a pariah, of course. They were there to make people well, and I was there, they knew, to make people talk. In between loads of wounded, the doctors, nurses and technicians would talk and fool around together. I would always stand by myself across the ER, the man in the black hat, as far as they were concerned. We never talked.

My letters home to my wife during this time showed the strain I was under. I seldom referred to my hospital duty directly, and I never described the daily bloodbath I was witnessing, but when I read those letters today, I can see them getting creepier by the day. Once I wrote twelve closely written pages on how nice it would be to fly to Mars and stay there. I speculated on what the weather must be like on a nice, clean planet like Mars and how wonderful it would be to lie out in the sun, so distant from filthy Earth. I was trying to cope, I guess, by mentally distancing myself from an awful job, one that exposed me to more pain and death than even an infantryman might see.

I was also fucking up on that job. My interrogation reports were routinely criticized by Captain Steele for incompleteness, overall incompetence, and sometimes incoherence. The army macho code, as well as my own private little war with Steele, dictated that I say nothing more than "No excuse, sir" when he did this. I kept promising to improve, but I found it increasingly difficult to keep my concentration. I felt I was slowly going crazy. On more than one occasion I would return to do a follow-up interrogation on a man I had seen in the ICU the day before and find that he had died the night before. Frequently, I found an empty bed in the ward where a live VC had been lying that morning. "Dead," the nurses would say, and go back to caring for the living. Once a suspected NVA sapper I was questioning closed his eyes and gave out a chilling throat rattle. "Dead," the nurse said when I called her over to examine him. She unhooked his tubes and called for an orderly. I had to tear up the report I was writing, wondering how I would excuse its incompleteness to Steele.

I continued my document duties, of course, and still conducted interrogations back at the IPW cage. Even as my abilities to handle hospital interrogations deteriorated, my confidence with unwounded prisoners and documents increased.

When the time came for me to be taken off hospital duty, I was replaced by three enlisted men. Steele had finally figured out that one person should never be allowed to face that much carnage day after day. I mentioned before that one of these replacements threw up in "my" bush outside the ER on the first day I took him on my rounds. Watching him pour the contents of his stomach into the bush, I remember thinking, Gee, the interrogators they're sending us these days sure are weaklings. After months in hell, I seemed to have forgotten how it would appear to a FNG. I brought the interrogator a paper towel and advised him to start wearing dark glasses.

"And don't bother talking to the chaplain," I said.

# CHAPTER 11

# Fast Times

As the brutal Vietnam summer blended into an almost imperceptible autumn, the varied kinds of work I was doing sorted themselves into a loosely knit schedule; I would spend most mornings at the hospital and most afternoons at my documents desk. The barely functioning document section I had inherited from Larry Hiller was growing and producing steadily. I now had two enlisted men, in addition to Larry, helping me handle the mounds of captured material. Office equipment had been expanded by some typewriters; a primitive, cranky copy machine; extra desks; and miscellaneous bins and boxes for incoming and outgoing paperwork. The section had become a going concern.

Senior officers who had never before been given access to enemy document information now greedily demanded it on a regular basis, and showed their pique when it didn't arrive fast enough. The Americal chief of staff, the G-2 officer, the MID commander, assistant chiefs of staff—all suddenly wanted to know what captured documents contained. I even received requests from MI battalion commanders stationed around the country, intelligence specialists at the 3d Marine Amphibious Force in Da Nang, and as far away as Long Binh, MI headquarters outside Saigon. One day in September, I received sixteen telephone calls, teletypes, or personal visits from nondivision sources, asking for document readouts or summaries. "It looks like you've transformed the IPW section into the documents section," Captain Steele remarked sarcastically that evening.

I was also experiencing the same problem I had when I

was the acting IPW section chief—dealing with superior officers. As a bottom-of-the-heap lieutenant, I simply could not speak to captains, majors, lieutenant colonels, and colonels with any confidence. Although I enjoyed a certain status as a document "expert," technically I was outranked by all of them and subject, within certain bounds, to their whims. Ironically, I was now beginning to get criticism of the system I had created from scratch. Either Captain Steele or I heard from irate staff officers with increasing frequency.

In the past, requests for captured document information went literally nowhere. Larry Hiller's job had been simply to play postal clerk for the documents, shipping them—unrecorded and unread—off to Saigon. Whatever calls for information that reached him were shuffled off to military limbo, unanswered. Now it was different. I made sure all document batches passing through my office were numbered, dated and entered into a crisp new logbook I bought at the PX. I knew precisely where every document was and in what stage of processing it happened to be. Some staff officers even presumed to tell me how to make the operation more efficient, proof of the old army saying "If it sits there, paint it; if it moves, supervise it."

Many of the documents we captured, especially the endless propaganda tracts, seemed to be of limited intelligence value. Others, like enemy unit rosters, personal letters, Communist association papers and orders from various VC and NVA commands, would become more useful after they had been joined together with similar documents and analyzed at the OB shop or the Combined Document Center in Saigon.

The surest sign of the success of my efforts came in September when I actually made the newspapers. Well, not me personally, but documents I had read out for the Americal Division. An article published in the Pacific *Stars and Stripes* and later syndicated widely in the United States ran with the frightening headline RED SUICIDE PLAN BARED. The lead paragraphs reported:

An enemy directive, calling for the organization of suicide teams in preparation for a third Communist offensive, was released Friday by the US Mission in Saigon. The directive instructs each village to set up at least one three-man suicide team "and prepare to infiltrate them into towns to assassinate tyrants and ring leaders." Dated Aug. 8 and carrying a "flash" priority, it was captured by a unit of the American Division in Quang Ngai Province.

I'm sure this sent chills up readers' spines as they recalled the suicidal Japanese kamikaze planes of World War II and fanatical Chinese human-wave assaults in Korea, but I'm afraid that the same just wasn't true for the Viet Cong. This "third offensive" document, the translation of which I oversaw personally, employed the term *cam-tu* to describe village infiltration teams. Literally—but only literally—translated, *cam-tu* does mean willing to die, but that is not its common connotation in Vietnamese. To the ordinary VC, and certainly to the author of the document, *cam-tu* implied "elite, prepared to fight hard." In other words, an eager, crack fighting team, but not one with a particularly strong death wish. After some discussion, my interpreter and the commander of the ARVN MID both agreed with me that a note of explanation on this inflammatory word should go to Saigon with the document translation to ensure that no one down there mistake its meaning and panic. The MACV press office and the American media apparently ignored our warning, and the suicide-squad article went out to editors and readers who believed it. Still, it was nice to see the Americal Division in print, and even nicer to realize that my obscure but efficient little documents sections was getting noticed.

About this time another lieutenant from the combat center, Mike Pojeski, reentered my life, and at an exceedingly awkward moment. It was just past 4:00 A.M., and I was drowsing in the command bunker of the Americal headquarters complex. Once a month or so I was required to perform a duty that devolved at some time on army junior officers all over the globe: officer of the guard. I had pulled this assignment only once back in the World, and that was at sleepy Biggs Field in El Paso. That time I spent the first half of the night chatting with my wife over the phone, and the other half tucked into a soft cot set up in the duty office for me. If anybody attacked us overnight, I never found out about it. My phone was busy, anyway.

At the Americal Division, it was different, of course. As officer of the guard, I was responsible for a line of manned bunkers placed between the central headquarters area and Highway 1. Twice during the night, I was required to drive the length of the bunker line and inspect each bunker for soldiers sleeping on guard duty. If we took fire, I was to telephone for help to an infantry company held in reserve, then alert higher headquarters. The usual wartime routine.

In the hours before dawn, after a full duty day and a night of cruising the bunker line, I found myself nodding off at my desk inside the command bunker. The sergeant of the guard, the enlisted man known as the "commander of the relief," and my duty driver were slumped over their desks, too, when Mike Pojeski strolled through the door, unannounced.

"Hi, Eric," he said, shaking my arm and disturbing the start of a wonderful dream about going home on an air-conditioned airliner.

"Jesus, Mike, what are you doing here?"

"I decided to take some time off from my platoon. I wanted to see the country a little. So I came to Chu Lai. They told me at the POW cage you were here."

Time off? What the hell did he mean. After the combat center, Mike had been assigned as a mortar platoon leader with the 196th Brigade at LZ Baldy, thirty or forty miles north of us. "Time off" without authorization meant "desertion," but gee, I could be judging too harshly here.

"I hitched a ride on Highway 1," he said in answer to my unspoken question.

Mike looked like shit. He wore no rank insignia and carried no weapon. His dusty fatigues were torn in places, and he wasn't wearing any boots or helmet. Since he was short, slight, and tanned from the tropical sun, you could almost mistake him for a Vietnamese.

"Come outside and talk," I said. The others in the bunker were staring at him, and I was getting slightly embarrassed. Mike was supposed to be an officer and a gentleman, after all.

He told me his plans. He was learning Vietnamese informally from ARVNs and interpreters at Baldy, and after he gave me a sampling of his linguistic progress, I concluded he could speak more fluently than I could at that point. He had decided to "adopt" an RF/PF unit (the Saigon government's answer to the VC—Regional Forces/Popular Forces stationed in friendly villages, called "Ruff-Puffs") and become an unofficial "advisor" to it. Where, he wondered, could he get his hands on some M-16s, new uniforms, and a deuce-and-a-half truck? "I'll be more valuable to the Ruff-Puffs if I come with equipment for everybody, don't you think, Eric?"

No doubt about it, Mike had become a Looney Tune up there at LZ Baldy. He had deserted his mortar unit, shucked his responsibilities, and was roaming around the countryside with delusions of becoming Vietnam's version of Lawrence of Arabia. Going native, as it were. He asked to spend the rest of the night, and then chose to curl up underneath my desk in the command bunker. "Rough day in the field," I remarked with what I hoped was nonchalance to the others, who were snickering at Mike's behavior.

He was gone without a word by the time my relief showed up at 7:00 A.M., but rumors of the crazy AWOL lieutenant filtered back to me over the next couple of days. I expected the MPs to arrest him immediately, but later, when I had been in country long enough to see more of this kind of thing, I realized that at any given time in Vietnam there were too many fruitcakes to control easily. People were flipping out with alarming regularity.

Two weeks or so later, Mike drove into the IPW compound just as I was about to go to evening chow. He was, by God, driving a deuce-and-a-half truck stuffed with C rations, rifles, shiny helmets, flak vests, and a pair of brand new .50-caliber machine guns still packed in their Cosmoline preservative. He was en route, he said, to equip and lead a Ruff-Puff unit near Duc Pho. I don't know how he acquired this stuff when my unit could hardly get new parts for a jeep in less than a month, and I don't know how he had avoided having a net thrown over him, but Mike Pojeski looked like he was going to carry out his insane plan in style.

After he drove off, Captain Steele called me over. "If I

were you, Smith, I wouldn't be seen with that guy. I hear he's under investigation for leaving his unit and dealing in the black market. A word to the wise."

Some investigation! At this rate Pojeski would be a general in the Ruff-Puffs before the army's rusty wheels of justice could grind an inch. But grind they did, and shortly after that, I ran into Mike at the division mess hall. He had been suspended from duty in the field (something he had already done for himself as far as I could see) but assigned as the PX officer for the Americal. I learned from a later experience that all officers under a shadow ended up with the PX-officer billet. It was a prelude to a court-martial and a quick trip out of the country. Mike was indeed stripped of his rank, drummed out of the army, and shipped home within a few weeks with a discharge for "mental instability."

Two combat center friends down, two to go.

Pojeski's bizarre behavior was no worse, in my opinion, than that of Lt. Col. Parker Deale, the prune-faced assistant G-2 for intelligence at the Americal Division. One of my many collateral duties during that part of my tour was to brief this man on behalf of the IPW section every evening at 5:00 P.M. The information I had to impart was relatively simple: the number and disposition of all POWs and CDs captured by the division during the previous twenty-four hours. No sweat—I merely had to call our subordinate brigade IPW sections over the telephone land line and ask for each day's totals.

Deale, however, had other ideas when I made my first appearance before him. "What did these prisoners have to say, Lieutenant Smith?"

"Excuse me, sir?"

"I mean, they didn't just sit on their fucking asses down at the brigades and say nothing all day, did they now? Didn't they have any military information to give?"

"Well, sir, I don't know. I didn't ask because I was getting the info over an unsecure land line, and I was told that no classified data could be relayed that way."

"Well think again, Lieutenant! I want some fucking goddamn answers tomorrow. I don't want just numbers, you hear?"

The next day I gave him the prisoner totals, and then I gave him a summary of the information extracted from them. He hit the roof.

"What's the matter with you? Are you *deaf*, Lieutenant? You're not supposed to get classified information over a land line. The VC could be listening in.'"

"But, sir, I don't have access to a secure hot line. I can only get the information over the field telephone."

"Bullshit! You get that information, and you get it the *right* way, you hear?"

"Yes, sir." I had no idea how to proceed. Then Lt. Bobby Biggers, a friend from language school days who had come to the Americal MID a few weeks before me, took me aside and told me in detail how to handle the crisis. "*This* is what Colonel Deale actually wants to hear, Eric . . ."

So the next day, I stood before scowling Colonel Deale, saluted smartly and said, "Nothing to report, sir."

He smiled slightly and said, "Fine. You can sit down, Lieutenant Smith."

This was preposterous, but it was exactly what my friend Biggers had told me would work. Colonel Deale had absolutely no interest in IPW information. He was probably aware of the communication problem that put any briefer like me in a bind, and he had no idea how to solve the problem, so what he really wanted from me was nothing— but nothing presented in an official way every day at 5:00 P.M. I was more than happy to comply. We were going to lose this war, anyway, so why bother my superiors with the facts?

Deale's abusive, inconsistent behavior was worse in its own way than Mike Pojeski's Lawrence of Vietnam act. But I encountered a lot of officers like Deale, usually majors and lieutenant colonels, in Vietnam. Now, with hindsight, I can see why they acted that way. Men holding these middle-management ranks had in most cases entered the army after the Korean War and enjoyed years of peacetime soldiering until Vietnam intruded inconveniently on their mid-life crises. They were used to the kind of spit-and-polish chickenshit that characterized duty in civilized places like Belgium and Fort Dix, New Jersey. A real shooting war with its endemic chaos confused and angered them and turned them sour. They hadn't a clue how to fight it, and thus took it out on junior officers who, because they were young and without preconceptions about what the "real" army should be, constantly challenged their authority and middle-aged view of warfare. It may not have been the only reason we fared so poorly in Vietnam, but it was one reason.

# CHAPTER 12

# Talking Heads

Interrogations, like lives, didn't always go the way you wanted them to go. The human element complicated what should otherwise have been a cut-and-dried process.

Like the reincarnation man, for instance.

This was an elderly Vietnamese gentleman who looked quite unremarkable standing among the scruffy villagers scooped up for questioning somewhere near Chu Lai. These people hadn't gone through any brigade screening, but were brought directly to the division POW cage on suspicion of being "possibly sympathetic to VC activities along the Tra Bong River," their capture tags said, whatever that all meant.

Fine. I and a few other interrogators would sort through this batch of obviously innocent civilians with some perfunctory questioning and be finished well before lunchtime. The elderly gentleman was my third subject that morning, and he looked so frail that I decided to get rid of him fast with a softball question.

"You're not VC, are you?" I asked with a smile, allowing him to deny it easily so he could exit gracefully.

He said, "I refuse to answer that," and clamped his mouth into a pugnacious, unyielding line.

"C'mon," I said, "you're too old to be scooting around the rice paddies with an AK-47 in your hands." He sat staring at me and didn't say a word.

"Look Mr., er, Nha," I said after looking at the name on his tag, "You're just making yourself look guilty by not talking. Are you VC or not?"

No response.

I wasn't sure Mr. Nha understood the consequences of keeping mum, so I asked my interpreter to have a private talk with him. The interpreter got exactly nowhere, so then I asked one of the female villagers I had already cleared to speak with him. She shrugged after five minutes of intense one-way conversation. "No talk," she said.

I was about to put stubborn Mr. Nha back in the cage for later questioning when he suddenly pointed at me. *"Toi se noi,"* he said, meaning he would speak, then he motioned me closer.

"Look here, young man," he said through my interpreter in a surprisingly vigorous voice, "I've decided to exchange a few words with you because you clearly don't understand something. I haven't the slightest fear of you or your entire army. Question me. Torture me. Pluck out my beard hairs one by one, I don't care. I've done nothing wrong, but that doesn't mean I have to answer silly questions from *anguoi My* (American) young enough to be my great-grandson."

"Why aren't you afraid of us?"

"Because I am a good Buddhist and have always been. I am a poor farmer in this life, as you can see, but since I have faithfully followed the noble Eightfold Path and believed in the Four Noble Truths, when I die and am reborn, I will be a rich farmer in my next life.

"So whatever you do to me, I couldn't care less. If you kill me, it will simply hasten my reward in the next life."

This was my first encounter with the teachings of Siddartha Gautama, who founded Buddhism in the sixth century B.C., as they were being interpreted by the unlettered country peasants of I Corps. Who knows, maybe Mr. Nha was right about his coming reincarnation? In any case, it got me off his back in his current incarnation—I released him that day with no further hectoring by any more ignorant young *nguoi My* like me.

And you never could tell. If I was good, maybe I would be a rich lieutenant in my next life.

Then there was that pretty girl in the hospital bed.

I was making my "rounds" (sounds almost like a doctor, doesn't it?) at the 312th Evac one morning with my interpreter, Sergeant Duy. Duy was a taciturn, pinch-faced fellow who seldom spoke outside of interrogation sessions. I suspected he was shy.

We stopped at a bed occupied by a young woman who had been only slightly wounded in the leg the day before. I passed her over earlier because I wanted to talk to the tough-looking, military-age men she had been evacuated with, but now I intended to find out how she happened to be among them while they were shooting at our soldiers. Duy and I sat on either side of her bed, down by her legs, and proceeded with a run-through of the EEI and other basic questions.

Her first responses were either grunts or mumbled monosyllables. Her follow-up responses were either two-word sentences or complete silence. She held her head down to her chest, not looking at us. Certainly she wasn't eager to talk.

As our interview went on, however, she brightened a bit and even began to volunteer answers before we asked any questions. In twenty minutes she was talking a blue streak. I couldn't keep up with my notes, so I asked Duy to slow her down. "I can't," he said with a rueful glance at the chattering girl. She was leaning forward out of her covers. Her beautiful eyes were sparkling, and her hands were fluttering. It occurred to me that she might actually be flirting with Duy, and he was just too bashful to control her rapidly accelerating gab.

But that wasn't the case. Not at all. After a half hour of this, Duy held his hand up to her mouth in a gesture commanding silence.

He turned to me and said "Lieutenant Smith, we have made a big mistake here. We should go. This girl has nothing valuable to say. She is merely exercising her mouth."

"But what the hell is she going on and on about, Duy?"

"You see, it's like this, Lieutenant. We Vietnamese men don't talk very much to our women. We expect them to understand a lot without us needing to use a lot of words. And we don't want them bothering us with too much talk. It is better that way, okay?

"But now this girl is actually being told to talk a lot. To you, of course, but also to me, a Vietnamese man—and a Vietnamese man who looks like he must listen to every word she speaks. And this Vietnamese man is actually taking notes on what she says. She finds this strange at first, but then she realizes she can say as much as she wants without being told to shut up. Now she is as happy as a butterfly, and now, Lieutenant Smith, she will talk about nothing but boring shit until the sun goes down tonight, okay? So let's go. I've had enough!"

We left. The girl was still talking as we walked out the ward door. I had learned a lesson in Vietnamese culture, but it wasn't one I could bring back to the World where the woman's liberation movement was quickly gaining momentum. Gloria Steinem would have just hated Sergeant Duy.

My schedule of hospital interrogations, POW cage interrogations, collateral duties (hootch maid control officer, war trophy screening officer, theft investigation officer, officer of the guard, and others), and document exploitation work was getting more hectic by the day. Most importantly, I noticed that I had a diminishing amount of time to do basic research before I talked to each prisoner.

This research was vital to my ability to tell whether a prisoner was lying or not. The information retrieval system that had been set up at the Americal MID was simple on paper, but nearly impossible to carry out. Technically, every interrogator was required to make a visit to the order of battle (OB) shop at the headquarters complex before conducting a prisoner interview. The OB shop was our "library" for all intents and purposes. Stored there were thick loose-leaf binders that contained all known information about VC and NVA units in our area: numerical designations, strength, names of officers (and some noncoms), weapons, training, last location, infiltration routes, unit history, tactics, food supply routes, base camps, health data—everything we could find out about our adversaries.

These unit books were of course based primarily on information gleaned from interrogations. After each interrogation report was turned in, my friend from language school (as well as my mentor at briefings), Bobby Biggers, and the rest of the OB shop crew would pore over it, extracting bits and pieces of information, inserting them into the unit book records and cross-referencing with other unit books. By the time I arrived in country, the Americal OB shop had an extensive, detailed library of unit books that presented a fairly clear picture of the forces we were facing out in the field.

This was the point at which mere information became actual intelligence. I had been taught at Fort Holabird that only after information had been collated and evaluated did it become "intelligence" per se. Those OB unit books were the sum total of what we knew, and for that reason they represented pure intelligence to me.

They had another important function, too. They could make interrogations a lot easier. At Fort Holabird, and again during my short-lived correspondence course on interrogation techniques at Fort Bliss, I learned that the best way to get a prisoner to reveal what he knew was to pretend that you already knew it. "I know that your sapper team is commanded by Quang and that two weeks ago you guys blew up an ARVN ammo dump outside Tam Ky City—so where did you obtain the C-4 plastic explosives to do it with?" is a typical leading question you should direct to a prisoner. It assumes great knowledge of the prisoner's unit on the part of the interrogator and should lead the prisoner to fess up. What the hell, the prisoner is supposed to think, this guy already knows we blew up the ammo dump, so I won't be giving much away if I tell him a few details. Besides, he will probably be able to tell if I'm lying because it looks like he knows everything anyway.

And that is exactly what the interrogator wants him to think, especially since the interrogator may not be at all sure about his information. "Knowledge is power" the saying goes, and it was never more true than during an interrogation. You can see, then, that the best possible preparation for an interrogation would be to go to the OB shop and bone up on the unit to which the prisoner you plan to see belongs. If you seem to know a lot about his unit, you can bamboozle him into spilling his guts about things you don't know about.

It was understood at the IPW section, therefore, that all interrogators would make a visit to the OB shop before talking to a prisoner for the first time. And in a perfect world, that system might have worked perfectly. Our circumstances, however, were far from ideal. For starters, our cage by the Chu Lai airfield was located miles from the OB shop at the Americal headquarters complex—too far to walk several times a day, and the OB people didn't make house calls. We could use jeeps to drive there, of course, but the IPW section possessed only three jeeps, and on any given day at least one would be redlined for repairs at the Americal motor pool (a swamp of inefficiency and delay into which jeeps disappeared for weeks at a time) and another wouldn't start for some reason. That often left us with only one jeep to ferry a dozen or more interrogators to and from the OB shop, and the remaining healthy jeep was needed for a myriad of other kinds of trips, too. In other words, we were chronically short of transportation.

What was the effect? Well, I began to notice that I was visiting the OB shop less and less frequently as time went on. I observed that the same was true for the other officers and the enlisted interrogators. We simply hadn't the time to wait for a jeep to become available or to hitchhike up to OB and still conduct the quota of interrogations that Captain Steele imposed on us. When the monsoon rains started up in midautumn 1968, all pretense of doing research at the OB shop was dropped. We were going into our interrogations blindfolded by a lack of information. Interrogations conducted that way, of course, produced information that was inferior because it hadn't been cross-checked with the OB books or evaluated in any way at all. Worse, this unverified information then found its way through reports into the unit books, where it mixed with previously gathered good information and tainted the entire product. After a few months of this, I felt I could no longer trust the accuracy of the intelligence I would find in the unit books, even assuming I had the time to check them.

This quickly became a vicious cycle in which the lack of "good" information produced "bad" information that became so polluted no one could use it, and so no one did. I was as guilty as anyone for this, but the realities of geography and machinery forced me to go along with it and hope for the best. Having already visited a brigade IPW operation, I knew that things were different there—scaled-down versions of information books on local VC and NVA units were compiled and retained by the brigade IPW team itself, so there was no OB shop involved and no need to travel to do research. It was just one more reason why I frequently daydreamed about being assigned to command a brigade interrogation team, even though I was afraid of being killed out there in the boondocks.

The final insult to my faith in our intelligence systems came while I was questioning a VC who belonged to the 48th Local Force Battalion (or so he said—I naturally hadn't bothered to check the OB books), a particularly wily and troublesome unit that had become the nemesis of the Americal Division. After a minimum of prompting, this wiry little fellow proudly told me that his entire company (about one hundred men) of the 48th had stepped out onto Highway 1 two nights before and marched right out in the open—in military formation, mind you—for nearly ten miles up the road before disappearing back into the brush. He had been captured the next day when he got separated from his company.

I could hardly believe him. The Americal routinely scanned that stretch of Highway 1 with side-looking airborne radar (SLAR) and airplane-mounted infrared light sensors. The best high-tech equipment money could buy. We also maintained a network of ARVN listening posts and guard stations all along this much-traveled route. There was absolutely no way on earth that one hundred armed VC soldiers could walk that road for even ten minutes and not be detected. Or was there?

This time I wanted answers. After finishing the interrogation, I hitchhiked up to MID headquarters and asked for all the SLAR, infrared, and listening post reports for that segment of the highway. It took a little time because I wasn't really cleared for information obtained by those means, but my friend Bobby Biggers convinced the elint nerds, hidden somewhere in an air-conditioned alcove, I imagined, that I had a need-to-know clearance for this. The reports all said that nothing unusual had been detected on Highway 1 on the night my detainee said he and his company strolled up the avenue in plain view of anyone who cared to look.

There wasn't much I could do about this disparity of opinion between the most sophisticated array of electronic devices ever employed in war and a local-yokel VC who couldn't even read a map. But I suspected that the VC was telling the truth. That kind of ballsy maneuver was typical of the smart-asses of the 48th, especially when I knew that they knew there was plenty of civilian foot traffic on Highway 1, even at night, to cover their movements. It was far more likely, I felt in my sinking heart, that a lot of tax money had been blown off on fancy electronic geegaws that just didn't work in the chaotic environment of Vietnam. And of course there was the real possibility of human error—a sleepy ARVN guard along the road, a moisture-induced gremlin in the SLAR, a sensor operator who was dreaming of his girl back home at the exact moment one hundred infrared heat sources showed up on his screen, or whatever.

The human element or not? Who knew? I only knew that someone, someday was going to have to rewrite the intelligence handbook back at Fort Holabird—and the first line of the first chapter should explain Murphy's Law in detail.

# CHAPTER 13

# Moody Blues

By the beginning of October, it had been raining for thirteen straight days.

In the early-morning monsoon gloom, I supervised an interrogator named Alvarez and his interpreter as they packed a jeep for our trip north. We were driving to a Vietnamese provincial hospital a few miles inland from the city of Tam Ky, forty miles up the coast from Chu Lai.

Two young women, daughters of a friendly village chief, had been captured by the VC five months earlier, then been summarily released. Dazed and probably malarial, they had wandered into a hospital after several days in open country. A U.S. Navy doctor attached to the medical staff there had alerted his headquarters, and in due course, the Americal MID found out about the women through channels. Like all of us, Captain Steele was eager to identify U.S. prisoners who might be out in the bush with VC units. Having spent several months with the VC on the move and in their base camps, these women could have had that kind of information and, because they were presumably still on our side, might be willing to share it with an interrogation team.

For reasons that were still unclear to me, Steele told me to go with the team to oversee the interrogation. This involved an eighty-mile round trip through relatively unsecure territory in an unarmed vehicle, so I was naturally nervous about going. It seemed to me that Alvarez and his interpreter could easily handle the women, but in those days I seldom questioned Steele's decisions. For some time, he and I had been getting along even more poorly than usual, and I couldn't help suspecting that he sent me out on missions like this simply to shake me up.

Packing our gear into the jeep made me smile; I could remember leaving on family trips back home, when my father supervised the loading of snack food, drink coolers, luggage, coats, and other travel paraphernalia. Today I was the "father," making sure Alvarez packed our flak jackets, maps, spare ammo, water can, rifles, .45 and .38 pistols, knives, and hand grenades. Hardly what you'd call packing for a picnic. We would be driving behind a convoy up to Tam Ky, but I wanted plenty of firepower on board in case we got separated from it. The trip up Highway 1 (a part of which became the Street Without Joy of Bernard Fall's influential book about Vietnam) was especially joyless in the monsoon downpour. Here is an excerpt from the letter I wrote my wife about the mission:

All the way along the highway were wooden hootches, little stone temples and thatched huts. It was 40 miles of unspeakable poverty—excrement and garbage was thrown into the slick, juicy mud and mixed into a Vietnamese cocktail of disgusting proportions and stench. Everywhere little brown kids waved at our jeep, catcalling and holding their hands out to beg from us. Most went naked and few had rain gear or even shirts.

Along the side of the highway, little bent women shuffled along, burdened with gigantic bundles and yolk-like carriers balanced over the shoulders and piled with pot shards, grass and foodstuffs. They were knee-deep in mud, and splattered with the refuse of countless trucks, buses and jeeps. The few adults we saw were only silent, dark, brooding faces glimpsed back in the dirty recesses of the huts. Most of the young men were probably dead or in the army.

The trip was completed without incident, and late that morning, we rolled up to the hospital, a long, single-story structure under a red tile roof. I saw lines of stretchers, most with wounded children on them, being carried inside. I remembered vaguely that elements of our 196th brigade were in contact with VC or NVA units over near Tam Ky, so I assumed all this activity must be the overflow of civilian casualties from the battle. The navy doctor met us outside and led us through the hospital to a back room where the women were being kept. This provincial hospital's "wards" were shockingly unlike those I was used to at the 312th Evac. Sanitation was almost nonexistent—floors were lavishly bloodstained and strewn with dirt, human feces, and castoff clothing. There was no electric light. The doctor himself looked like he had passed the point of exhaustion, and his forearms were streaked with mud and dried blood.

In the back room, palely lit by an unglassed window, the two women ignored our arrival. Both had shaven heads (for lice, the doctor said before leaving us alone with them) and eyes unnaturally enlarged in sunken sockets. The older one, about twenty-three I guessed, sat on the edge of a cot, rocking herself and nodding her head slowly. She was mumbling what the interpreter confirmed were nonsense words and phrases. The younger woman, barely out of her teens, stood stark still on the filthy floor, staring vacantly into space.

The preliminary report we had heard back at division indicated that the women had been used by the VC as manual laborers and constant blood donors for wounded VC. There was also evidence they had been abused sexually. I had no idea how this information had been obtained, because neither woman would speak to us. Their emaciated appearance and severely withdrawn manner lent credence to the report, however. It looked to me, in fact, like they had both been driven insane by their five-month ordeal. Speaking gently, Alvarez and I tried to put the women at ease by offering them cigarettes (the universal Vietnamese sign of friendship) and even the few candy bars we had brought along, but none of it seemed to work.

Although the standing woman would only stare straight ahead, the one seated on the cot occasionally looked up from her rocking and mumbling to throw us what looked for all the world like a coquettish smile. In a bizarre, ironic imitation of the bar girls and country whores we had seen, this woman appeared to be flirting with us through her haze of shock and malnutrition. "Let's go," I said to Alvarez and the interpreter, "there's nothing here for us."

On our way out, I found the doctor and asked if the women had come in with documents of any kind. "No, but the young one did write something on a piece of paper after she got here," he said.

"Can I see it?"

"Sure, Lieutenant, I've got it right here. But it's just one word, and I don't even know what it means."

I handed the scrap of rice paper to the interpreter. "Can you translate?"

He looked down at the word, neatly written in ballpoint pen, then up at me. "The word is 'vengeance,' sir."

I thanked the doctor, who hurried away to another line of stretchers full of children, and walked over to the jeep. "Let's get the fuck out of here. Please," I said to Alvarez and the interpreter.

Back in Chu Lai, my mood of depression deepened. The incessant monsoon rains were likely to continue for months. I was painfully lonely for my wife and weary of going to sleep every night wondering if a rocket or mortar round would extend my night's rest indefinitely. Captain Steele seemed to go out of his way either to ignore me or dispatch me on shitty, pointless missions like the one to the hospital. When we spoke, it was brief and unpleasant, with him taking every opportunity to criticize my interrogation reports, my military bearing (of which I had little, I admit) and my general drag-ass attitude. And as I mentioned before, I was taking increasing heat from senior officers about the efficiency of the valuable but still imperfect document process I had created. I made little social contact with anyone in the base camp and never went to the Chu Lai officers club at night. I was becoming such a recluse that I even stopped eating at the mess halls available to the IPW section. In order to eat, I picked up a case of C rations from a mess sergeant and took to cooking them on a one-burner electric stove in my hootch. Actually, the C rations tasted better than the mess hall food.

I also fought a running personality battle with my hootch mate, Lieutenant Buttroon, who finally became so hostile that he constructed a thatched wall between our bunk areas. I ripped the first one down because it interfered with my ability to exit the hootch fast during rocket attacks, but he

built another, less intrusive one after that. Daily hospital interrogations were wearing me down, too, but then who
wouldn't get depressed working in a charnel house? My letters to my wife grew ever crazier.

One drizzly afternoon in October, when I thought I had
reached the bottom of my personal pit, an incident took
place that reminded me, temporarily, of how far down I had
to go to become truly nuts. A captain over in the CI section, a West Point graduate and in every visible way a normal, competent officer, decided that the war in Vietnam
was over for him. He stripped down to his army skivvies,
walked out the door of the CI office, and climbed into the
back of a deuce-and-a-half truck.

"I'm not coming out until I'm sent home," he told one
of the enlisted men. "This war is fucked up, and I won't
participate any more." His first tour of duty after graduation
had been in nice, peaceful Germany, where he apparently
had discharged his duties without incident. This was his
first exposure to combat duty, and probably his last.

The captain's presence in the back of the truck was duly
reported to the CI commander, Captain Roma, who
promptly (and typically) bucked this unexpected personnel
problem up the line. For the next day or two, a procession
of ever more senior officers up to the rank of colonel visited the CI section and asked to speak to the loony in the
truck. They tried reasoning with him, offering to forget the
incident if he resumed his duties. Then they tried ordering
him out of the truck, but that didn't work, either.

During this time, I brought some of my spare C rations
over to the captain, out of pity. He accepted my offerings,
cheerfully, while squatting behind the truck's loading gate
in his underpants. "I'm going home, I know it," he said to
me often.

He was right. After a while some medics from the 312th
Evac drove down to coax the captain out of the truck.
They didn't exactly throw a net over him, but the effect
was the same; he went off in their jeep, smiling and waving to the onlookers. As it happened, I was the only on-
looker. For a moment, I envied the poor son of a bitch.

While I was at the Americal IPW section, I never knew
how many prisoners I had interrogated or how many docu-

ments I processed. These were not factory jobs, after all, and "production" numbers seemed irrelevant at the time. Curiosity about my output caught up with me years later, however, so I wrote away to the Department of Defense for any information it could provide about the activities of the Americal Division in those days. After much exchanging of paperwork with DOD and its allied agencies, I received in the mail one day some bundles of badly Xeroxed documents and a tiny envelope of microfiche.

These were what passed for the "history" (unclassified) of my division during my tour of duty between the summer of 1968 and the spring of 1969—a loose compilation of papers entitled "Operational Reports—Lessons Learned." Scanning through the material, I found the following entry under the October 31, 1968, quarterly report for the IPW portion of the G-2/MID section:

> Although the MID was not formally organized and personnel shortages remained, the quality and timeliness of intelligence information produced was markedly improved. Interrogation and document translation reports were revised and expanded to provide a more complete and clear intelligence document. 30,000 pages of captured enemy documents were processed.

Captain Steele had probably written that passage. It sounded like his inelegant armyese.

Well, well, so I plowed through thirty thousand pages, did I? It would have been nice if Steele had mentioned the name of his lowly document exploitation officer in connection with that number, especially since I was also responsible for the "revised and expanded" document reports he was discreetly bragging about. I was interested, too, to see that the IPW section was short of personnel in those dark monsoon days. It occurred to me, after many years of stewing about Steele's apparent unfairness to me, that he kept sending me outside the base camp on missions simply because no one else was available to do it. Could he have sent the timorous, ass-kissing Lieutenant Buttroon? I wouldn't have if I had been in his place. Buttroon was an office pet, not a field animal. How about Lt. Tom Guggenschaffer?

Not likely. Tom's mind was on going home, and you don't put someone who's getting short out in the field—as a matter of combat-zone courtesy, and because short-timers are dangerously edgy. IPW got a couple of new lieutenants in while I was there, but they were too green to go beyond the wire for quite a while.

So who did that leave? Me, I guess. Steele was forced to rely on the lieutenant he disliked the most, the "snotty, drag-ass ROTC kid," for his outside missions. That must have frustrated him no end, although he could always console himself with the thought that I might not come back alive the next time. I swear, sometimes I was ferociously motivated to return to Chu Lai just to see the disappointment in Steele's eyes, but perhaps I'm being paranoid here. It's no wonder, then, that Steele didn't mention my name in his October report—despite my modest successes with documents and prisoners, I was the obnoxious guest who wouldn't leave.

Soon, though, I would be out of Steele's close-cropped hair, at least for a little while.

# CHAPTER 14

# Gone South

Call it a mission if you'd like.

Or call it a "courier flight," as our orders to Saigon said.

But Bobby Biggers and I called it a junket, pure and simple.

The whole thing was his idea in the first place. After one of our afternoon briefings of the onion-faced assistant G-2 (at which I reported, "Nothing to report, sir," for the umpteenth time), Bobby, the deputy OB officer as well as my old friend from language school, approached me with his plan. "Listen, Eric, most of our buddies from Fort Bliss are down in Saigon now, right?"

"Yeah. We seem to be the only ones to have gotten stuck in a hole like this."

"Just my point. They're down there sipping champagne with gorgeous hookers and sleeping in villas while we're up here getting rocketed every night and eating Colonel Deale's shit every day. So what do you say we go down there and visit them?"

"You mean fly to Saigon?" To me he might as well have suggested flying to Uranus.

"Exactly. We'll go as couriers, with official orders and everything. Just for a few days, or course. But we'll have a goddam blast down there."

"Bobby, just how in hell do you think you're going to arrange this . . . this junket?"

"Leave it to me. This is Bobby Biggers you're talkin' to, remember?" His good-ole-boy accent got thicker with his plotting.

But he was as good as his promise. Using the headquarters connections he had forged at the OB shop, where every officer in the Americal intelligence community had to come for help, he wangled a set of orders sending us to Saigon and back within a four-day period the following week. Officially we would be carrying dispatches, correspondence, and classified documents to the Combined Military Interrogation Center (CMIC); after we turned them in, however, we would be free to party with our buddies who, as chance would have it, were all working at CMIC.

For once, Captain Steele was inclined to be semi-indulgent when I told him about the plan. "Good idea, Smith. While you're in Saigon, though, I've got some things for you to do." What he asked seemed easy enough: I was to pick up a new copying machine that he would order in advance and bring it back to Chu Lai, and I was to make an inspection visit to the Combined Document Exploitation Center (CDEC), which was supposed to be the most sophisticated computer operation of its kind in Vietnam. The "Combined" in CDEC and CMIC referred to their joint operation by U.S. and South Vietnamese personnel. It actually sounded kind of interesting, and I was sure I could spare some time left over from carousing with my friends to see it.

A week later, Bobby and I were strapped to the bench seats in the back of a C-130 cargo plane, headed four hundred miles south to Saigon, the "Pearl of the Orient." Two of our CMIC friends met us when we landed at Tan Son Nhut airport and drove us back into the city. Saigon in the late fall of 1968 was at the height of its power, beauty, and corruption. The road from the airport was bordered with teeming slums of squatter's shacks made from tin sheeting, cardboard, and bits of castoff military equipment, but the city itself had retained much of its charming mix of French and Oriental architecture. Signs of the war were everywhere, of course; it had only been ten months since the Tet Offensive brought VC sapper squads into the heart of Saigon. Every tree-lined boulevard had its concrete crash barriers and machine-gun posts, and rifle-toting soldiers seemed to outnumber the civilian population in places.

I was a bit awestruck, as it had been nearly a year since

I had been in a city of any size. Like a country bumpkin on the town, I gawked at the white Presidential Palace, the monuments, the tawdry bars on Tu Do Street, and the almost unbelievably beautiful women walking in their bright *ao-dai* dresses. Street vendors, most of them blatant black marketeers, called temptations out to us from underneath the old French balconies. It was difficult to believe that Saigon and the shitty little village of An Tan near Chu Lai belonged to the same country.

Bobby and I had left Chu Lai armed, of course. As a headquarters type, he carried only a .45 pistol, but I took along my M-1 carbine as well as a snub-nosed .38 revolver on the trip. Our friend at the wheel of the jeep slowed down as he approached the gate of the CMIC building complex, and when he stopped, a brown arm emerged suddenly from the guard box—it was reaching for the barrel of my carbine, slung over my right shoulder. Without thinking, I yanked my weapon out of the clutching hand and slammed its buttstock into the face of the man behind the arm. This is what I would have done if any Vietnamese back at my base camp had ever made such a move to disarm me.

It was not, however, what Saigon soldiers were supposed to do, and I found that out when my friend yelled "Jesus, Eric! Quit it, you asshole!" I was already out of the jeep, leveling the barrel of my carbine at the man, who was lying on the ground and rubbing his jaw. I wasn't going to shoot him, though, just ask him nicely what the fuck he was doing. My friend picked up the man, who I could now see was an ARVN military policeman, and explained quickly to me that all Americans were required to turn in their weapons at the gate. Some sort of rule about unauthorized firearms in the city. I felt very stupid for not realizing that the guard was merely collecting my weapon until I left the compound, and apologized to the man as far as my Vietnamese would go.

"Christ, Eric, we can dress you up, but we can't take you out," my friend laughed, apparently forgiving me for my uncivilized manners.

"I guess I've been out in the boondocks too long," I replied with my face burning.

"Boy, you really are. You and Bobby are up there in the shit, the field. It must really suck."

"Well, you know, it's not that bad, only a division base camp. The guys lower down the chain at brigade, or the battalion fire support bases—now they're the ones in the real shit."

My friend looked at me. "Are you kidding? If any of us here at CMIC have to go visit a division base camp—and it doesn't happen often, thank God—we consider that field duty. Dangerous stuff."

It was clear from this conversation that the definition of "the field" differed with a person's perspective. Relatively speaking, a division base camp is downtown Manhattan compared with a brigade base camp, and so on down the line until everyone would agree that the grunt sleeping out at night with monsoon rain in his face is, at last, in the real "field." But to my Saigon friend, surrounded by urban comforts and forbidden to carry a rifle, I looked like a dirt-streaked country cousin indeed. It all reminded me that I really wanted to get out of the division MID, despite its relative comfort, and be assigned to a level closer to the actual field—a brigade IPW team. I made a mental note to start sniffing around for such an assignment when I returned to Chu Lai.

Bobby and I had a delightful reunion with our language school classmates. We shook hands and clapped each other on the back vigorously (these were the days before hugging between men) and took jokingly critical looks at each other to see what changes our time in Vietnam had wrought. Bobby and I had lost the most weight (I dropped twenty pounds from sheer nervousness in just my first two weeks in country), and our CMIC friends had gained some since we had all last been together in El Paso. One man's wife was pregnant, obviously from a farewell burst of semen, and another's wife had written him a "Dear John" letter. The usual ebb and flow. They took Bobby and me outside to watch their regular afternoon softball game on a lush grass field, and later they escorted us over to a palatial officers club called the Seven Oceans or something like that. I had my first genuine U.S.-type beef hamburger in months and got slightly tipsy on expensive Scotch. Later that night, in our friends' billet, I was disappointed to find that the hot shower I had been looking forward to was only a lukewarm trickle from a mildewed shower head. Saigon villa living wasn't all it was cracked up to be.

The next day Bobby and I and a few of our off-duty friends hit the famous Cholon marketplace and wandered around the stalls for a while. In the Cholon PX, which was stuffed with frenzied South Korean soldiers buying up everything in sight, I bought a pair of jade earrings to mail home to my wife for Christmas. It would be a long time before I would see her wearing them.

After all the small talk and catching-up chatter with our friends, Bobby and I turned the conversation to the jobs they were doing at CMIC. This was the ultimate destination for some of the more valuable prisoners I had questioned up in Chu Lai, and I was curious about the methods used in Saigon to extract more information out of them. Did they use torture? High-tech verification methods? Sophisticated interrogation techniques? My CMIC friends were hesitant to answer. They made vague references to need-to-know categories and information clearances higher than the top secret clearances Bobby and I had been given. It was clear after a while that our friends considered us too low on the intelligence totem pole to share information with. We were out of the loop, and it might be breaking regulations to talk with us about these subjects. Ironically, I wouldn't even be allowed to hear about prisoners I had sent to Saigon myself only weeks before. So much for the MI brotherhood.

Early on that second day in Saigon, I had called ahead for an appointment to visit CDEC and been told to show up at the center, near Tan Son Nhut airbase, at about 2:00 P.M. Right on time, I was standing outside the front door of the CDEC building. A friendly young captain who had been assigned as my escort took me into a large room that looked like it was wallpapered with computers. Back then, long before computer terminals became a part of every home and office landscape, it looked to me like a "Star Trek" set. The CDEC captain was obviously proud of the system he worked with, and he took extra time to explain its intricacies to me. I don't remember all the details now, but I do remember actually getting excited about document exploitation for the first time since I had taken on the job up at the Americal.

Now this was a system anybody could love. The captain

explained that every single document I had mailed to CDEC (along with millions of documents from other divisions, of course) was translated, summarized, and indexed by rooms full of interpreters and analysts. The data was keypunched onto index cards and filed in an interfacing network of IBM computers along with the original Vietnamese document. Facts dealing with the VC or NVA forces or political infrastructure were collated and cross-referenced inside the computers before being transferred to microfilm strips.

To gain access to all this information, the captain said, all you had to do was ask "the answer machine," which in effect was the room full of computers we were standing in. "Go ahead, ask it anything you want," the captain said.

Oh, yes. This was an intelligence dream come true, a document officer's Disneyland. Let's see . . . what did I want to know? My mind clogged up immediately with disorganized questions and random bits of data, so I chose a trivial but, I thought, difficult to answer query: what was the average age of junior VC lieutenants in the 48th Local Force Battalion, the nemesis of the Americal? "No problem," the captain said. He typed my question onto a card and inserted it in a slot located next to what looked like a TV screen. Then he pressed a button. The screen came alive with blurry images as strips of microfilm streaked by. "This baby will sort through more than five thousand pages a minute," he said. We stared at the screen in mutual fascination.

Every so often the screen images stopped moving and a document would be frozen in the frame. Another button was pressed, and a photocopy of that document would flop into a tray below the screen. In ten minutes the tray was stacked with document reproductions, each containing information that contributed in some way to the final answer. The last piece of paper into the tray said "Average age/ junior lieutenants/48th Local Force Battalion/Chu Lai AOR: 19 years."

"Holy shit!" was all I could manage in reply. The captain smiled. "Try a few more questions, but I have to get back to work pretty soon, okay?" "Yes sir," I said, and settled down to another half hour or so of happily playing the CDEC version of a computer game. The captain finally

walked me to the door, chuckling at the obvious happy daze
I was in. "It would be nice if someday they came up with
a way to get machines like this out to the divisions," he
said, returning my salute and my handshake. "Oh, God, I
wish," I said, not realizing at the time how close both of us
almost were to having those wishes granted.

Years later, I was asked to sit on the board of my alma
mater's library support group. I attended the first meeting
on Georgetown's campus in Washington and met a distinguished older gentleman who was introduced to me as a
former army intelligence general. "I was in MI, too," I told
him, "but only as a lieutenant." The conversation pro-
gressed to talk of our respective duties in Vietnam, and at
one point, I mentioned how impressed I had been with this
computer system I had once seen at CDEC in Saigon.
"What do you know about that," he said, "I designed that
system. Well, not the computer hardware, but the information retrieval system. That was my specialty within MI—
getting information into a format where it could be used.
The CDEC operation was my brainchild."

"You created that?" I grabbed his hand and pumped it
hard. "I swear to God, General, that's the only thing I ever
saw in Vietnam that worked."

"Yes, and if the war hadn't slowed down in '69 and '70,
and the money hadn't dried up, I would have been able to
afford to export my CDEC system to the divisions out in
the field. I was planning to have trucks with satellite dishes
mounted on the top and computer hookups inside so document officers anywhere in Vietnam could access all that
wonderful data we had in Saigon."

His eyes twinkled and so did mine as my mind roamed
gleefully over the possibilities. I imagined myself back in
Vietnam, sitting in an air-conditioned truck and playing
with a keyboard that could call up the answers to any question I could conceive about the VC and NVA forces in our
area. What a fantastic tool it would have been.

I spent my last evening in Saigon playing a very odd volleyball game at the CMIC complex. My friends there had
told me earlier that MI didn't actually own the buildings used
for interrogations. They were rented—that's right, rented—
from the ARVN authorities, so the American tenants always

had to be diplomatic whenever they dealt with their touchy Vietnamese landlords. During the periodic volleyball games between the U.S. and ARVN personnel stationed at CMIC, for example, it would have been considered bad form for the taller, more aggressive Americans to beat their ARVN opponents too often or too decisively. To make sure that didn't happen, an MI lieutenant colonel, whose job it was to control the rate of play, was always placed in the middle of the U.S. team formation. With his whistle and stage-whispered commands, he ensured that U.S. players blew their serves, spikes, and setups often enough to lose. That way ARVN honor was preserved, and so was the delicate balance of landlord-tenant power at CMIC. Once during the game, I lost my head and scored an unauthorized point at the net. That earned me a glare and a short lecture from the lieutenant colonel on the niceties of losing.

Frankly, I was glad to leave Saigon with Bobby the next morning. So many strange Vietnamese milling around everywhere made me nervous, and I missed the comforting weight of a pistol holster around my waist or a carbine in my hand. In a way I even felt sorry for my CMIC friends. If you're going to fight a war, I thought, you might as well fight it in a warlike environment instead of the Vietnamese version of New York City. My friends were cloistered, disarmed, and compelled to play chicken games of volleyball in the name of diplomacy. True, they were coddled and a lot safer than I was at dirty old Chu Lai, but I found myself anticipating my return to the Americal with a kind of subdued pleasure. Be it ever so humble, and all that.

After I left the captain at CDEC, I had gone to another part of the building to pick up the photocopier Captain Steele wanted. I lugged the damn bulky thing all the way back to Chu Lai, but it didn't make a single copy at the IPW section. Much of our electricity there was produced from a nearby gas-powered generator, and as a result, our power levels fluctuated wildly. The poor copy machine never even got enough juice to start up, much less work smoothly. The last time I remember seeing it before leaving the division IPW section, it was sitting in a corner under a dust-coated cover. Technology was always an iffy proposition in Vietnam.

# CHAPTER 15

# Public Relations

By the time I got back to Chu Lai, I was all pumped up about the value of captured documents. Seeing the classy operations at CDEC inspired me, at least for a while, to work harder and more creatively at this aspect of my job.

One way to "succeed" at document exploitation was to have your readouts reprinted in one of the general intelligence publications circulated around Vietnam. The two I knew best were the intelligence summary and the periodic intelligence report, known in armyese as the "intsum" and "perintrep," respectively. Although these reports were classified confidential and not intended for everyone's eyes, they still functioned as unofficial newspapers for the intelligence community in Vietnam.

The intsum and the perintrep provided isolated document officers like me with a peek at what others were doing in places like Da Nang, Dalat, Qui Nhon, Tuy Hoa, Pleiku, and Vung Tau in the other three corps areas. The reports provided a forum for sharing information, tips, and items of interest among people who were doing the same job all over Vietnam—watching Charlie to figure out what he would do next. A month before my visit to Saigon, I noticed an enemy document readout printed in the latest perintrep that had been supervised by a language school classmate who had become the document officer for the 101st Airborne Division. I admit I was a little jealous of him. Making the perintrep bestowed a certain amount of status on my friend—his name was being circulated all over the country, and the very presence of his readout in the perintrep implied that he had scored an intelligence coup of some sort. In fact, his document contained information of only minor interest, yet I envied even the mundane celebrity he had achieved.

How, I wondered, could I get one of my own document readouts into the perintrep? The opportunity came one afternoon soon after I returned to Chu Lai.

I was glancing over a set of instructions to pro-VC villagers written by a member of the Communist political infrastructure. Even through the ARVN translator's awkward phrasing, I could see the mind of a desk-bound VC bureaucrat at work, trying to keep up the morale of loyal villagers after the failure of a recent "Third Offensive" in I Corps to drive the Americans back into the sea. I remembered that offensive as a couple of uncoordinated rocket attacks on Chu Lai and not much else. It was also the one that caused the "suicide-squad" scare in U.S. newspapers for a while, a scare the media hyped up after the Saigon press office mistranslated my document readout.

In any case, the offensive flopped, and now some VC chair jockey had a bright idea for the downcast villagers: "Great Brothers in the Struggle against American Revanchist Imperialism," the document in my hand said, "THIS time we must fight even harder than before and we must use All Means to counter the American Dog's bombing. From now on, all villagers will, during bomb attacks, remain in the center of the village—eating rice and singing to drown out the sound of the bomb explosions."

I read these amazing words again to make sure I had them right. Was this guy actually suggesting that villagers stay in the open and eat while they were being bombed? And sing, too? He certainly was, and good luck to any peasants idiotic enough to listen to him. I always believed that the Pentagon in Washington had cornered the market in bonehead military bureaucrats, but this incredible document proved that the VC way out here in I Corps employed them, too.

Now this, I thought, could be an interesting item for the next perintrep. Not a particularly valuable item, you understand, but an amusing one. I had learned by now that offbeat or downright bizarre reports like this attracted a lot of attention from the brass and earned space in the perintreps and intsums. Like civilian readers of newspapers back home, the brass hats in Vietnam often confused exciting items with important ones. Really useful intelligence, in fact, is quite the opposite: dull, low-level, and repetitious. But mine was not to reason why—merely to get my name in the perintrep. Accordingly, I typed up a long and fancy report on this outrageous document, passed it up through MI channels and waited for the result.

Not surprisingly, my report made the front page of the next perintrep, and suddenly, I was a minor celebrity around the MID. I received a lot of "Good work, Lieutenant," and "Excellent report, Smith," comments from various senior officers. Even the dour Captain Steele felt compelled to make begrudging congratulatory noises at me. The fact that this totally absurd item was of no real intelligence value seemed to have escaped everyone's notice. Earlier reports I had submitted to the perintrep on dull topics like infiltration routes or ammunition supplies had been ignored, but ironically I could make a reputation as a crackerjack document officer on one silly scoop about singing villagers. As a journalist today, I understand the natural appeal of the strange, the horrifying, and the ridiculous to newspaper readers, and I do my best to give it to them frequently. But it was back in Vietnam that I first discovered the secret of getting published.

Every once in a while, however, I got to earn my pay with a truly valuable document readout. A few weeks after I returned from the Saigon trip, a document packet taken off a recently captured member of the local VC infrastructure came across my desk. The ARVN translator's summary directed my attention to a letter from the local VC headquarters to the prisoner, instructing him to show up at a certain hamlet near Chu Lai for an important meeting of the area's political cadre. The letter was gratifyingly specific about the date, time, and exact location of the meeting, which was to be held only four days hence. I sensed an opportunity here, so I took out some maps and plotted the most probable site of the meeting, a low hilltop two miles west of Chu Lai, as it was described in the letter.

Then I walked over to the CI section, whose responsibilities included the VC infrastructure, and conferred with some agents there. We quickly formulated a plan and went up to MID headquarters with it. It was unusual for any direct action to be taken as a result of document information, but this, we felt, was an exception, and the MID commander agreed with us. He made appropriate arrangements with the Americal Division artillery headquarters at Chu Lai, and four days later, at the time and place designated in the letter, a large number of high-explosive 155mm artillery rounds descended on the meeting site. The CI people had sent one of their Vietnamese agents out to observe, and a day later, he came back to report an outcome that surpassed our highest hopes—right on target, the shells had exploded in the midst of the VC meeting and killed or severely wounded eight participants outright. Dazed by the unexpected artillery raid, the three or four survivors immediately assumed that one of their number had betrayed the group. Our observer, who had been hiding nearby, said that an argument then broke out, ending in a wild gunfight at close range that caused at least two more casualties. Apparently no one had taken the time to figure that the only man who didn't come to the meeting (now our prisoner) could have been the traitor, accidental or otherwise. Anyway, it was one VC infrastructure meeting that was forced to adjourn early, and that was one document readout I would never forget.

In addition to scheming my way into a perintrep or two, I also found another way to get published, albeit on a much humbler level. It started when I drew a small sketch to illustrate one of my interrogation reports. The prisoner had traveled all over Quang Ngai and Quang Nam Provinces before we picked him up. His route was too complicated to recount in words alone, so I pulled out a mimeograph stencil and detailed his precapture journeys in the form of an impromptu map. To make it more visually appealing as well as accurate, I added a few flourishes of cross-hatching and shading on hill and river areas. This wasn't particularly hard to do since I had been drawing for school publications, and later my hometown paper, for years. I had been the staff cartoonist for my high school and college newspapers, and if all went well I planned to become at least a part-time illustrator in the future (those plans worked out so well that I have now been a professional cartoonist and illustrator since 1972).

At the time, however, I didn't think too much about my little sketch map. I had it reproduced on the office mimeo machine and appended it to the distribution copies of my interrogation report. The response surprised me. In short order I was being asked by other interrogators to illustrate portions of their reports—maps of infiltration routes and jungle base camps at first, and then more complicated renderings of VC weapons, uniforms, insignia, miscellaneous equipment, and odd things like field-expedient kitchens. Because they had a chronic supply problem, the VC often jury-rigged their own versions of mines, grenades, and bits of field gear they couldn't obtain through channels. The best example of this was the Ho Chi Minh sandal contrived by VC guerrillas from castoff U.S. tires. I frequently wore a pair myself around the IPW compound.

From prisoners' descriptions, I was able to depict these items clearly enough for analysts up the line to glean some intelligence value from them. Or at least I hoped so. In any case, I was able to put my embryonic drawing talent to work and enjoy doing the work at the same time. From then on, my mimeo stencil sketches were a regular feature of many of our interrogation reports. Even Captain Steele, whose macho mentality made him suspicious of any artistic endeavor, conceded that illustrations "improved the product." A real art critic, that man.

December 1968 arrived, and with it came the long-awaited "reorganization" of the disorganized Americal Division. Junior officers like me were of course too far down on the division's organizational chart to be privy to, or even understand, the high-level command-and-control changes that were scheduled to take place. As I mentioned before, it all had something to do with the fact that the Americal dribbled into Vietnam in bits and pieces, collectively labeled Task Force Oregon, in late 1966 and early 1967. Eventually the task force sorted itself into three maneuver brigades and a home base camp placed along a sixty-plus-mile stretch of South China Sea coastline between Da Nang and Quang Ngai Province. But the individ-

ual brigades had been allowed to become too independent
for the increasingly structured war we were fighting in
Vietnam, and it was time to haul in the reins.

Accordingly, every command within the division made
plans to consolidate its administrative hold on subordinate
units out in the countryside by the end of December 1968.
To the MID, that meant disbanding the old brigade intelligence detachments and reforming them as MI "teams"
(MITs) under tighter supervision by Chu Lai. Most of the
changes were made only on paper and were purely seman-
tic or cosmetic. Lieutenants still commanded the brigade
teams, and the teams were still composed of interrogators,
interpreters, clerks, and counterintelligence agents. Their
jobs were still the same, too—find out what Charlie was up
to and tell everyone who needed to know. The only real
difference would be that the brigade MIT commanders
(now called "officers in charge," or OICs) would answer
directly to Captain Steele at the division IPW section, and
ultimately to the major (a new arrival named Lee) who ran
the MID at Chu Lai.

Even so, the brigade teams, formerly on their own, relatively speaking, had to be taught who was boss under the
new plan. Somebody at the division MID came up with the
bright idea that all vehicles belonging to the brigade intelligence detachments should be brought back to Chu Lai—
and then immediately be reassigned back to the brigades.
This would be a demonstration of the division MID's power
to taketh away and giveth back, or so the eggheads at division believed. It would also give headquarters at Chu Lai a
chance to inventory the all-important jeeps and trucks and
repair or replace them if necessary. The plan was discussed,
approved, and set for execution sometime in mid-
December. As far as I know, nobody sought the opinions of
the brigade lieutenants on this matter, which could mean a
monstrous inconvenience for them. This was an oversight
for which I would soon suffer.

I was only mildly surprised when Captain Steele walked
into my hootch after duty hours (a time he always seemed
to reserve for unpleasant orders to me) on December 9, and
with his customary brusqueness brought up the subject of a
convoy. "Lieutenant Smith, I want you to go down to Duc

Pho tomorrow and bring all the intelligence detachment vehicles back to Chu Lai for reassignment."

"What time do I have to leave tomorrow, sir?" I wasted no time on protests or professions of ignorance of what he was talking about. I had heard rumors of a move like this for months.

"I've got a Chinook ready to leave at 0500," he said. He then sat in one of the two beat-up lawn chairs I had commandeered for my hootch and outlined the plan: I was to take twenty men with me in a big Chinook troop helicopter to Duc Pho, the place to which I had made my first trip outside the base camp months ago; my detachment would include a few *chieu hois* (turncoat VC who had agreed to work for our side), but the rest would be enlisted clerks and interrogators from the division IPW section—in other words, not exactly a combat-hardened outfit. Most of these guys wore thick glasses (like me) and spent their days flattening their butts on office chairs.

We were to take possession of all seven vehicles—jeeps, three-quarter-ton and two-and-a-half-ton trucks—belonging to the 11th Brigade intelligence team and drive them approximately thirty miles north back to Chu Lai on Highway 1 by the end of the day. Everyone would be supplied with M-16 rifles, flak vests, and full combat gear for the trip. "It's a standard convoy operation," Steele said.

"But I've never done a convoy before, sir." I felt like adding that I didn't do windows either. "Are there any special procedures?"

"Here, I got a transportation corps manual on convoy organization," he said, throwing the book onto my bunk. "Just read over it, and you should be ready by tomorrow morning."

Right.

I don't mind a bit admitting that my stomach dropped into my boots when I heard all this. With almost no warning, Steele was sending me out with a bunch of inexperienced paper-pushers and traitorous former enemy soldiers to traverse the country's most dangerous road in one hellish day. And all I had to help me was a dog-eared transportation corps manual.

While one of the young sergeants coming with me

rounded up the detachment for the next morning, I paid a visit to the hootch of my best friend, a warrant officer my age who worked at MID headquarters. "Will you be my second-in-command for this? I need some help bad," I said. "Sorry, Eric," he replied, "friendship is one thing, but a convoy through VC territory is another. There's no fuckin' way I'm ever going to leave this base camp." So, after a nearly sleepless night poring over the manual, I arose well before dawn the next morning and met my ragtag little detachment at the IPW chopper pad. I was nervous to the point of pissing until my prick had the dry heaves, of course.

We disembarked from the Chinook at LZ Liz, the 11th Brigade's main chopper pad, and hiked over to the POW cage. There I was met by an extremely hostile lieutenant in charge. "You assholes from division are gonna take all my vehicles away, huh?" he said. "Don't worry," I told him, "you'll get them back in a day or two. This is just reorganization chickenshit." Still, he refused to give me any spare tires or cans of water for the vehicles until I called back to Captain Steele and asked him to order the truculent lieutenant to do so. I wasn't going to take a joyride over thirty unsecured miles of lumpy, shell-pocked road without extra tires and water for radiators that were sure to overheat on the way.

I also checked in with the brigade artillery officer, as the manual said I should do, to arrange for fire support along the convoy route. We went over the map of Highway 1, selecting a number of natural and man-made features (hilltops, road-drainage culverts, etc.) that should be visible to me once I got out onto the highway. These would be the registration points, marked by eight-digit coordinates and labeled on both our maps, that the artillery commander and I would use as common references. If my convoy was ambushed and I wanted support fire, I was to call back to Duc Pho on a preset radio frequency (my command jeep was equipped with a medium-range PRC-25 radio) and ask for three spotting rounds of Willie Peter, or white phosphorous explosives, on top of the nearest numbered reference point. Once I saw the large white clouds of smoke appear from the impacts, I could adjust fire onto any nearby target by calling in corrections in increments of fifty yards.

In theory it was a good system. I was worried, however, that if I needed artillery help fast, my fear and inexperience would cause me to foul it up. As things turned out, my worst fears were justified.

Then I assembled my convoy detachment by the vehicles to give some last-minute instructions. "Remember, if we come under fire out there, you should keep driving straight ahead. Do not, I repeat, do not stop for any reason unless I order otherwise." I explained that the VC set up ambush kill zones into which they concentrated their aim. A vehicle that braked to a stop under fire merely prolonged the time it was vulnerable. I told them that if a vehicle became disabled during an ambush, the crew should abandon it and jump onto the next vehicle coming through. In fact, I hadn't the faintest fucking idea of what might actually befall a convoy full of greenhorns that was being shot at, but I did my best to improvise my instructions with common sense and hints from the maddeningly vague transportation corps manual. I also checked with each driver to make sure his vehicle had extra water cans, at least one spare tire, and plenty of ammo for the man riding shotgun. Some of the vehicles, including my command jeep, had an extra guard in the person of one of the *chieu hoi* scouts we brought with us. The one in my jeep had taken along three or four extra M-16s, which he piled in the back seat and fussed over until we left.

I had been told that a mine-sweeping team from the 11th Brigade was routinely sent out every morning to clear the first few miles of Highway 1 outside Duc Pho. After that it was purely a matter of luck if you didn't hit a VC mine. For this trip, though, we were getting extra protection from a military police scout car that would accompany us as far as Quang Ngai City, about seventeen miles north of Duc Pho.

All was in readiness except my bladder, which kept producing nervous jets of urine right up to our departure time. At 10:00 A.M. I was told that the mine-sweeping team had finished, and we could go. I wished everyone luck and told them we would stop for our first road break at Quang Ngai.

I climbed into the right-hand seat of my jeep at the tail end of the column (which is where the manual said it should be, despite the well-known fact that VC ambushes concentrated on the first and last vehicles in a convoy) and waved my arm, "Let's move it out!" I shouted. Under my breath, I mumbled the Lord's Prayer to myself.

Five minutes out of Duc Pho, I heard the first shot. Just a single round, probably from a rifle. It came from the right side of the road, which at that point was closely bordered with vegetation. I heard a few more scattered shots, then the distinctive report of an automatic weapon. Oh, shit.

As the column of vehicles ahead began to slow down (in violation of my instructions not a half hour before), I saw plumes of blue cordite gunsmoke pouring out of the bushes and trees by the roadside. This had every appearance of an ambush, but I couldn't see if bullets were hitting the vehicles or the road ahead. Brake lights on the trucks and jeeps in front began to pop on, and some of the vehicles were swerving slightly from the drivers' pressure on their steering wheels. Grinning like a pirate, the ex-VC scout in the back of my jeep hauled out one of his M-16s and let loose with a couple of rounds toward the smoke. My driver turned to me and yelled, "What do we do now, Lieutenant Smith?"

This was the age-old question junior officers feared the most, the one we were told repeatedly in training we would certainly hear some day from one of our men, and the one we had damn well better be ready for. It was the moment of truth. It was also the moment I completely crapped out.

Here's all I can remember of what happened in the next minute or so. I ripped open the flap of my holster, drew my .45 and discharged one or two ineffective rounds into the trees beside the jeep. I grabbed the radio handset and made babbling noises into it, some of which might have been the correct ones to identify myself and request artillery support, but who knows? The problem was I couldn't recognize any registration points nearby, mainly because I couldn't see anything but walls of green on both sides of the road. None of the other convoy vehicles had a radio, so I couldn't communicate with them while we were strung out along the road like this. Then I tried to think fast: if we stopped immediately, we would escape being hit by gunfire, but I would look like a total coward; if we speeded up, we would enter the kill zone along with the rest of the convoy and probably be blown away. Suddenly I felt the inadequacy of my flak jacket, which offered no armor protection for the sides, and that was where the bullets would be coming from.

The most important question, however, was whether we were actually being ambushed or not. Was this a VC unit shooting at us? Was the firing coming from some other unit, U.S. or ARVN? Could this other unit possibly be facing away from the road, engaging in a skirmish with another adversary? Why was I seeing smoke and hearing shots, but not seeing any effect of the gunfire? Was somebody merely conducting target practice near the road? My mind had thrown itself into such confusion that I couldn't make a clear judgment. It was all happening so fast—shots, smoke, braking vehicles, and that horrible question from my driver. Up ahead, I saw the MP scout car, which was supposed to be guarding us, accelerate ahead of the convoy and disappear around a turn. So much for our extra protection.

I had to make a choice. "Keep going!" I yelled to the driver, and that, folks, was the last thing I remember.

My next memory was a series of impressions that came all at once. I wasn't sitting in the jeep any more, I was standing next to it on the right side. I looked around—the convoy was intact and had parked by the shoulder of the road just ahead of the jeep. My driver was serenely smoking a cigarette, and the scout in back was napping. Behind the jeep, through clouds of road dust thrown up by passing vehicles, I could see the unmistakable cityscape of the provincial capital of Quang Ngai, about fifteen miles north of the "ambush" site.

Clearly something odd was going on.

I looked at my watch: it was 1:00 P.M., three hours after our departure from Duc Pho and two hours and fifty-five minutes after I had heard the first shot beside Highway 1. I was now holding the radio handset, apparently in the middle of a conversation with the commander of a convoy out of Quang Ngai. I remembered that Captain Steele had arranged for us to link up with this convoy and proceed up to Chu Lai together if we made it to Quang Ngai on time.

The other convoy's lead vehicle was coming into sight, so I instructed the commander to pull in ahead of us for the ride back to the division base camp.

But what the hell had happened? Everything looked normal. No casualties, no bullet, grenade, or rocket damage to any vehicles that I could see (I examined them all carefully after we got back and found nothing but road grime). Could I have imagined the whole "ambush" sequence? Was I having a bout with malaria? Had I gone stark, raving nuts? If I had, there was no sign that anyone else in the convoy thought so. My driver wasn't staring at me, and at no time did any of the other members of the detachment treat me as if I had flipped out. I debated asking my driver about the incident back at Duc Pho, but since he was acting as if nothing had happened, I was too embarrassed to raise the issue. I was supposed to be an officer, after all, and I couldn't just ask one of my men under my command, "Say, can you tell me if we all survived an ambush back there?" or "Excuse me, have I been curled up in a fetal position for the last three hours, crying for my mother because I heard (or imagined I heard) some gunshots?"

No, that wouldn't do at all. I just kept my mouth shut and finished out the convoy in company with the vehicles we picked up at Quang Ngai. About ten miles farther up Highway 1 a few mortar rounds exploded on the road fifty yards behind us, but all the vehicles speeded up without prompting from me, and we drove on without any trouble. The shells might or might not have come from an ambushing VC unit, but by this time I couldn't tell who was shooting at whom or why. The trip became so boring, especially after we left behind the dirt portion of Highway 1 and drove onto a paved surface, that I idly checked the map to see how many of my artillery registration points I could recognize. The answer was none. Years of combat and convoy traffic had obliterated all of the road intersections and culverts I had so laboriously marked on my outdated map. Hillsides and other natural features near the road could have been changed by wartime construction, and I realized too late that my inexperienced eyes couldn't tell one hilltop from another, anyway. My fancy artillery support preparation had been a bust. I also found out later that my ammo check before the convoy's departure had been a bust too: the men had neglected to examine the boxes of ammo that the irate 11th Brigade lieutenant had provided for each vehicle—my men were armed with M-16 rifles, but the boxes contained ammunition for the M-14, a rifle no one but rear-area Marines used any more. It's just a good thing we didn't get into a firefight.

We drove through the gates of Chu Lai, parked our vehicles by the IPW compound and disbanded. A week later those same trucks and jeeps would be returned to the 11th Brigade team, but that would be some other convoy commander's job. I made a verbal report to Captain Steele, remembering not to mention the "ambush" until I had a chance to sort out the day's events, and made a beeline for the volleyball court for the regular evening game. The warm sand under my feet and sea breeze on my grimy face had never, ever felt so wonderful. Whether my life had been in danger of being snuffed out or not, it was good to be alive on that December day.

I never brought up the "ambush" again while I was in Vietnam, and no one else did, either. Years later I spoke to a psychologist about my interrupted memory of that day, and she gave several possible explanations—the most plausible one being that the shock of hearing those first shots in a combat environment caused me to "block" all conscious memory of that period. Based on the normal way the men treated me later, I most probably did not do or say anything obviously strange. I may even have continued to issue orders and behave appropriately until we reached Quang Ngai. I still don't know where those shots came from. Some local VC may have decided to take a few random, poorly aimed potshots at us as we passed by, or the gunfire may have indeed come from a nearby U.S. or ARVN unit shooting at something else altogether.

I'll never know. It was my first commmand under combat conditions, and I guess I can forgive myself for getting a traumatic case of jitters. Over the next months, I would become a little more accustomed to doing my job while being shot at, but the truth is that I never really got used to being scared out of my wits.

# CHAPTER 16

## Peace on Earth

Jingle bells, mortar shells
Charlie's in the grass.
Take your Merry Christmas
And shove it up your ass.

This was a sour little Christmas carol that made the rounds of the Americal Division as the holidays approached. It was the latter part of December 1968, and back in the World people were putting up trees, finishing off their Christmas shopping, and planning parties with each other. It was the season to celebrate peace on earth, goodwill toward men, and joyous reunions with families and loved ones.

In grim, monsoon-soaked I Corps, of course, it was the other way around. No peace, zero goodwill, and a depressing absence of loved ones. Even on Christmas morning, I would be doing interrogations and poring over documents that had been taken from dead men's pockets.

Still, there was always the Bob Hope show. We had been hearing rumors that the famed entertainer, who had been visiting troops in the field since World War II, might actually be making a stopover in Chu Lai. I had thought that the giant marine complex up in Da Nang would be the closest a protected Hollywood luminary like Bob Hope would be allowed to come, but speculation said he could indeed be with us for the holidays. In an odd sort of way, seeing Bob Hope in person would validate my wartime experience. I would know that I was not just having a prolonged bad dream, but that I was actually overseas, far from home in a combat zone, if a smiling, joking Bob Hope came like jolly old Santa Claus to visit on Christmas.

Another sign of the approaching holiday was a Christmas card I received from the local Viet Cong. Well, it wasn't exactly a greeting card, but it was a genuine greeting, and it did come to me through regular army postal channels, by God. Here is what I found in my IPW mail slot a week before Christmas: a small leaflet printed on cheap paper, entitled "Xmas 68-PA PA COME HOME." A crude line drawing depicted a typical American family sitting around the dining room table. Not one, but two Christmas trees stood in the background (I guess the VC wanted to emphasize their point). The mother was crying, however, because there was only a big question mark shown over the chair where the father, obviously a U.S. soldier in Vietnam, should have been sitting. The message said, "How your parents, wives and children miss you on Christmas eve and wait for your return." On the back side it said, "A merry Christmas, A happy new year to those whose conscience is clear and wish all U.S. troops to withdraw from South Vietnam." It was signed "The Quang nam province National front for Liberation."

A cheery Yuletide thought from the enemy. Now wasn't that sweet. What disturbed me, though, was that it somehow made it through our internal mail distribution system. No one else at the IPW section had received the leaflet, so I assumed that it was targeted for me alone. Had it been slipped into my mail slot by someone inside the base camp? Had it been "mailed" from a nearby village and incorporated into that day's mail call? I would never know, despite a few inquiries I made with our interpreters and over at the ARVN detachment. I got chuckles and head shakes for answers, but no hint about the method used to slip the leaflet to me. Apparently some intelligence type at the Quang Nam Liberation Front office knew more about me than I did about him—a situation that seemed to prevail all over the country. It was one more reminder of how little we knew about our adversaries in Vietnam.

Now that I had played my small part in the reorganization of the division, I wondered if the new regimen would affect my job prospects. After six months of being close to the flagpole at the division IPW section, I was eager to get away into the field in some capacity. There were too many nosy, demanding senior officers hanging around Chu Lai for my comfort. Every move I made was hemmed in by bureaucratic routine, chickenshit regulations, and questioning superiors. As the United States poured more and more troops into the Vietnam conflict, the Americal Division began filling up with excess command baggage. New levels of supervision added new levels of rules, procedures, and inspections. Paperwork at IPW proliferated to the point where even Captain Steele grumbled that it reminded him of the spit-and-polish Stateside military duty he thought he left behind.

One incident brought this home to me. A few days before Christmas, I was walking near the hospital after an interrogation when I saw a jeep approaching me on the road. It was packed with men, and I paid no attention when it passed by. Suddenly the jeep braked to a halt, and a first lieutenant wearing starched fatigues separated himself from the passenger group and strode briefly back to where I was standing.

"What is your name and unit?" he demanded, pulling out a pad and pencil.

"Who wants to know?" I didn't feel like being friendly to someone of my own rank who looked and sounded like a hall monitor from high school.

"You failed to salute the general's jeep, and the general wants to report it to your commanding officer," he said.

"You mean there's a big brass hat in there somewhere?"

"There certainly is," he sniffed. "That fact is patently indicated by the license plate marked with white stars on a red field that is mounted on the front of the jeep. You obviously ignored it."

I explained that I had never seen a general's jeep before and had no idea it was supposed to be saluted. That was the kind of crap I expected back at Fort Benning, not in a combat zone. The lieutenant, who was clearly the general's aide and all-purpose bird dog, was having none of it, however. He wrote down my name and unit and admonished me for my ignorant lack of military courtesy. In return, I told him he was a dick-sucking, ass-kissing slimeball who should be ashamed of himself for hassling an honest soldier. We parted frostily, and the next day the MID commander gave me an obligatory dressing-down for mouthing off as well as overlooking the general's jeep.

But you see what I mean. The traditional army bureaucracy, held temporarily in check by the exigencies of an overseas war, was beginning to reestablish its choke hold in Chu Lai and probably all over Vietnam by then. It was past time to get out. The fastest way out for me was to get a command slot down at one of the three brigade MITs, yet so far I had heard nothing about that kind of assignment. In my heart, too, I was still afraid of leaving the comforting, if often smothering, bosom of division duty. The old dilemma was still there, and I had no power to resolve it. Soon enough, however, it would be resolved for me.

Christmas Eve finally came, and with it a short respite from the war. I arose early that morning and went for a swim on the beach below the IPW compound. The ocean was cold, and it was an annoyance to traverse the tangles of concertina wire and concrete abutments to reach the water, but I felt refreshed afterwards. An IPW outdoor barbecue was scheduled for late afternoon, right after the Bob Hope show, which had in fact stopped over at Chu Lai. It was held on a wooden stage set in a natural bowl between two hillocks down by the South China Sea. Security choppers hovered overhead, and navy ships patrolled beyond the tide line. Troops from all over the division operations area had been given leave to visit Chu Lai to see the show. I wondered if the VC contemplated launching an attack at a time when our forward positions were undermanned like that, but then I realized that even the VC hadn't had enough time to plan for action—no one knew for sure that Bob Hope was coming until the day before.

The show itself was both invigorating and depressing. Knowing that troops in the field love cheesecake, Hope had brought along a troupe of American beauties like Ann-Margret and the Golddiggers all-girl singing group. It pained my heart (and my crotch) to see these gorgeous round-eyed women cavorting on the stage, wiggling every body part they owned for our collective titillation. We

couldn't have them; they knew we couldn't have them, and
having them so close but untouchable was as frustrating as
it was entertaining. Hope cracked some obligatory jokes
about the army and the VC forces around Chu Lai, but for
some reason concentrated his humor on the recent seizure
of the American spy ship *Pueblo* by North Korea. Frankly
I couldn't give a damn about the situation in Korea when
I was ass-deep in my own Asian conflict, but Hope seemed
to think many of us would. I had remembered to bring the
little camera my wife gave me before I left, but I had then
forgotten to bring extra film. I ran out of pictures just before Bob Hope walked onstage, and so today I show friends
photos of an empty stage and say, "This is the Bob Hope
Show without Bob Hope."

The barbecue back at IPW was a delight—fresh steaks,
corn on the cob, salad, potatoes, and plenty of alcohol. The
day was overcast and chilly, which reminded me of home
during the Christmas season. For a short time, I forgot my
chronic depression and dislike of many of my colleagues
and entered into the holiday spirit—a spirit that was only
slightly dampened when the neighboring VC picked that
time to lob several mortar rounds and rockets into Chu Lai.
They were probably showing their resentment for not getting to see the Golddiggers.

My wife and family had nearly overwhelmed the
Americal post office with boxes of presents for me. Two
precious jeeps had to be sent to pick them up. Inside one
of the boxes was an artificial Christmas tree from my wife,
who had obviously forgotten my letters describing the ever-
green trees all around the IPW compound. I assembled the
tree late Christmas Eve and placed my brightly wrapped
presents around it. I would open them after the interrogation I was scheduled to perform the next morning. Very
early on Christmas Day, I walked into the POW cage with
my interpreter, who was groggy from the celebrations the
day before, and sat down across the table from my detainee.
I felt that I should say something special to him on this ho-
liest of holidays, so through my interpreter I addressed him
as follows: "Merry Christmas, you little gook motherfucker,
and what is the numerical designation of your unit?"

A week later, on New Year's Eve, I got really drunk for

the first time. At one point, early in the festivities, I climbed to the top of a hootch and performed what everyone told me later was a perfect half gainer into the volleyball net. As midnight approached, however, the effects of my earlier drinking wore off slightly and were replaced by the frequent urge to vomit. By 11:45, I was almost ready to flop into bed, but one of the interrogators, who had served a tour in Vietnam two years before, told me I could see the "fireworks" if I went to the top of a sand dune at the edge of the compound.

Expecting at best a few feeble firecrackers and roman candles, I stood at the brow of the dune and waited calmly for midnight. Ignorant me.

"Get down, you asshole!" someone yelled at me from below.

"What for?" I asked.

"You'll see in a minute. Take cover, damn it!"

I squatted down and put on my helmet, and then the whole world erupted in my face.

At the stroke of midnight (remember, the army loves to synchronize watches), what seemed like every weapon in the drunken hands of some fifteen thousand men was fired off. The sky turned a sickly orange with pulsing streams of tracer bullets. Plumes of Willie Peter shells exploded overhead. Flares of all colors popped into the air from every corner of the base camp. Marine pilots took off from the Chu Lai airstrip in F-4 Phantom jets and hosed the nearby mountain slopes with rockets and machine gun fire, and then released all their bombs at once. Helicopter gunships lurched into the sky and lit it up with electric-powered miniguns and 20mm cannons.

Down on the ground, infantrymen and clerks discharged M-16 rifles along with pistols, mortars, machine guns, rocket launchers, recoilless rifles, tank guns, and M-79 grenade launchers. Not to be outdone, the American's artillery batteries crammed star shells and high-explosive rounds into their howitzers and shot them off as fast as they could. Over at the navy compound in Chu Lai harbor, ship crews let loose with all their heavy weapons. When the wild shooting stopped, I sat up, dazed from the blasting and brilliant bursts of light. Now that was a great New Year's show.

The next morning a VC sapper named Pham Van Duong was brought into the POW cage for interrogation. He had been the point man for an assault squad that had been planning to break into the division compound the night before. His hands were still clutched around a pair of wire cutters, and his eyes were glazed with fright. It took us an hour or so to calm him down and get his story, which was that at approximately thirty seconds to midnight, he had squirmed into position to place his cutters on the outermost string of Chu Lai's barbed-wire defenses. All was quiet, but at the precise moment he clamped down on the wire, the entire Americal Division apparently woke up and began shooting.

This poor devil thought he had set off the biggest, loudest alarm in military history.

No one had ever told him about the good old American custom of making noise on New Year's Eve. His fellow sappers took off in a panic and left little Duong on the wire, but we explained it all to him before shipping him off to a permanent prison camp.

# CHAPTER 17

# Transition Phase

The army called it R & R, which stood for rest and re-cuperation leave, and each soldier was entitled to one of these breaks during his Vietnam tour. After more than seven months in country, I was more than ready for it. My wife and I had decided that I would take the allotted six-day R & R period sometime after the halfway point in my tour, which turned out to be mid-January 1969. We also decided to meet in Hawaii, where most of the married soldiers went. Single guys looking to blow off emotional and sexual steam usually chose to be flown to different places around the Far East, like Bangkok, Hong Kong, and even Austra-lia. There they would often rent a prostitute for a week, drink to joyful excess, catch a few tourist sights, and come back to Vietnam exhausted and hung over, but happy.

I had of course received a letter from my wife nearly ev-ery day, but I had only heard her voice once since I left her at the Knoxville airport the previous July. That was when I called her at the end of August through the MARS network (Military Affiliate Radio System), an overseas radiotele-phone link set up for soldiers in Vietnam with the help of volunteer ham operators. Although MARS was a well-intentioned system, it was not a satisfactory one. I had to reserve a calling time with both my wife and the army sev-eral days in advance, and then wait around for hours for my turn to enter the little wooden building at division head-quarters that held the telephone handset. You were in-structed to say "over" after every conversational break, and so you found yourself saying ridiculous things like, "I miss you and wish like hell I could be there to kiss your breasts. Over." My wife's voice was so garbled by the static that it didn't even sound like her, and she reported in a letter that at least half the words I said during our five-minute conversation were inaudible. I never tried it again. It was too painful.

While I was at division headquarters one day a couple of weeks before I went to Hawaii, I ran into another of the lieutenants I had become friendly with back at the combat center. He was Phil Talbott, a taciturn, heavy-set National Guard officer from somewhere in the Midwest who had volunteered for (or been called into, I can't recall which) Vietnam service. I saw him in the division mess hall at lunchtime, and when he sat with me for a minute, he said he had been withdrawn from infantry duty in the field to be the PX officer. Uh-oh, I thought, not again. Mike Pojeski, my other friend from the combat center, had been assigned as the "PX officer" just before the army court-martialed him and sent him home in disgrace. Now Talbott was holding down the same billet. Did that mean he was in trouble, too?

I didn't see him again after that, but I didn't have to wait very long for an answer. Two weeks later I took the freedom bird flight down to Cam Ranh Bay and was on an R & R flight to Honolulu the next morning. The plane stopped over on the island of Guam to refuel for about an hour, so I walked into the little air terminal to stretch my legs. On one of the waiting room chairs lay a copy of the *Overseas Weekly*, a commercial (i.e., non-army) newspaper whose audience was GIs and their families; it circulated without official permission throughout the Pacific theater. I never saw a copy in Chu Lai, but I had heard that this publication regularly embarrassed the military establishment with its irreverent stories and antiwar tone. Smoothing the mildewed trousers of my khaki uniform, I sat down eagerly to examine this forbidden journalism fruit.

On one of the back pages I found a reprint of portions of the transcript of Phil Talbott's court-martial, which had convened in Chu Lai about a week before. Phil had been charged with rape and sodomy with a thirteen-year-old Vietnamese girl. He had been found guilty by the army tribunal and sentenced to five years hard labor in the military prison in Fort Leavenworth, Kansas. According to the *Overseas Weekly* story that ran with the transcript excerpts, the senior sergeant in Phil's infantry platoon had suspected for some time that his commanding officer was committing frequent sex crimes in the local villages. Early one evening, he followed Phil into the hamlet bordering the platoon's night encampment and arrested him at gunpoint while he was in the process of raping and sodomizing a barely pubescent girl. My own reading of the account of this incident led me to believe that the sergeant may have used this arrest to revenge other, unreported grievances against his officer, but the fact remained that Phil had been caught, literally, with his pants down in a brutal, criminal act. No wonder he had seemed so subdued at the division mess hall—he was facing a trial within days.

Three down now: Warren Witzener had lost an arm; Mike Pojeski had lost his mind; Phil Talbott had just lost his freedom. Only the lieutenant I remembered as "the Indian" and I remained unscathed so far from the original combat center group. In a perverted sort of way, I was keeping score on our dissolution. As of the moment in the air terminal on Guam, dissolution was winning, three to two.

My plane arrived at the airport on Oahu shortly before 5:00 A.M., and by 5:30 the buses waiting for us had broken all speed limits to deliver us to the reception building on the grounds of Fort DeRussey in downtown Honolulu. It was a bizarre scene that awaited us; in the predawn darkness, we spilled out of the buses and into a huge, brightly lit room, lined on both sides with silent, tensely waiting women. One by one, the men ahead of me were snatched up by their wives and sucked into the crowd. I walked hesitantly down the aisle between the women, hoping my wife would pick me out of the line. A flowered lei suddenly dropped around my shoulders, smooth white arms encircled my neck, and I found myself being kissed ferociously by a woman I didn't recognize. I pulled back, afraid that some overeager wife had made a mistake, but it *was* JanElaine, my own wife. After so many months of trying to remember her face, I found that she now looked nothing like my memories. It was like kissing a vaguely familiar stranger. She later confessed to me that she checked out the name tag on my wrinkled uniform just before she grabbed me, to make sure. I had lost a lot of weight, and I guess my face showed some outward signs of strain, too. At that point, we had been married for less time than we had been separated.

Our five days in Hawaii rocketed by. We slept late, ate greedily, and took in the tourist attractions between long walks on Waikiki Beach. We saw Sea World and Pearl Harbor and swam on the secluded beach at Bellows Air Force Base. We shopped for tropical fruits in the supermarket and illegally picked pineapples from the Dole fields along the road. We went on picnics among the volcanic rocks and made love by the surf. We planned for the future, although secretly I didn't believe I was going to survive my tour. I reveled in air-conditioning, hot showers, gargantuan breakfasts, and the feel of a civilian car's steering wheel under my hands (a rented Datsun). JanElaine and I talked for hours on end, hungry for each other's company.

And then it was time to fly back to Vietnam.

I had just climbed out of the jeep IPW had sent to pick me up at the Chu Lai airfield when Captain Steele said, "I want to see you in my office."

"Can it wait until I unpack and change into my fatigues, sir?"

"Now."

In his office, he handed me a folder of papers. "It's your OER. Read it and sign it before you give it back to me. Dismissed."

I walked over to my documents desk in the adjacent hootch and opened the folder. It was my Officer Efficiency Report, the first one I was due for since I had come on active duty. The OER, we were told from the beginning of ROTC training back at Georgetown, could make or break an officer's career. If you received a bad or even below-average rating from your commanding officer on your first assessment as a lieutenant, you could kiss any chances of making general good-bye. In fact, you might just as well get out of the army if you fucked up as a junior officer. I had no immediate intention of staying in the service, mainly because it would mean another combat tour within a year or two, but I wanted to keep my options open.

My OER was a disaster. That would account for Steele's brusque manner.

In it he had written (in so many words) that I was immature, ornery, rebellious, and slow to carry out even the simplest order. He mentioned that I had accumulated seven—count them, seven—uniform violations on my record, which I might add was not easy to do in a combat zone where regulations were lax. My failure to salute the general's jeep was noted in there, too. Steele made no mention of my ground-breaking document efforts, the bloody hospital interrogations I had to endure, or any of the missions I had performed outside the base camp. I was a shitty soldier in his eyes, and that was that.

I hate to admit it, but he was right. Despite doing a lot of work I was proud of, my general attitude toward the army, Vietnam, and Captain Steele was decidedly negative, and it showed. Those childhood daydreams I used to have about being an inspiring leader in a war someday had been pulverized by gritty reality. I had to face the fact that I was not John Wayne, but Sad Sack.

This was my lowest point by far—aching homesickness left over from Hawaii, gruesome months left to go in my tour, and on top of it all a confidence-smashing OER. My only consolation was that the army couldn't punish me by sending me to Vietnam because I was already there. I signed the report and returned it to Captain Steele in his office without comment. "You know, you're not a total disaster as an officer, Smith, but you've got to get your shit together," he said, perhaps because he felt a little guilty. I simply saluted him and walked out.

I went to a movie that night. It was shown, as always, at the Marine Corps officers club, located a short walk down the beach from the IPW compound. The Marines were there to man a set of Hawk surface-to-air missile batteries, and I always felt kind of sorry for them because they had nothing to do all day long but prepare for North Vietnamese warplanes that would never come. Maybe it was the uselessness of their mission that caused the Marine officers to party so strenuously in their club every evening. The movie that night, and for about the hundredth night in a row, was *The Spy with the Green Hat,* starring Robert Vaughn from the "Man from U.N.C.L.E." television series and a scrumptious but forgettable Italian starlet named Eva Renzi. By now, I knew this grade B film, apparently the only one in the Marine film library, so intimately that I could recite most of its tepid dialogue by heart, so I paid little attention while I nursed a Coke at a beer-stained table by myself.

Lieutenant Buttroon ambled over and pulled up a chair next to me. I ignored him on the grounds that I might be forced to share a hootch with that festering asshole, but I sure didn't have to socialize with him. He was wearing a fey little grin, which I knew from past experience meant he had a secret to impart. "There's a rumor going around that you're going to get a brigade slot. Real soon," he said.

I hadn't heard that, and even if such a rumor was in the air it must be inoperable now because of my slime-sucking OER. "What're you talking about?" I growled.

"You remember Lieutenant McDodge over at the 198th? Well, I heard that they're bringing him back here to do some shit job."

I was gazing intently at the screen now. After watching dozens of repetitions of this predictable potboiler, I knew that Eva Renzi was about to show some leg. "Yeah, so?" I said to Buttroon over my shoulder.

"Well, you're supposed to be replacing McDodge. I heard Captain Steele talking about it with the MID commander."

That got my attention at last. Lieutenant McDodge was the OIC of the intelligence team, MIT #3, at the 198th Infantry Brigade, the guard brigade for the division. Its scruffy little base camp, LZ Bayonet, was down Highway 1, a few miles south and west of Chu Lai. If the rumor was indeed true, that McDodge was out and I was in, my whole Vietnam career was about to change drastically.

The rumor was true.

The next afternoon, Captain Steele summoned me to his office. Major Lee, the new MID commander, was sitting by Steele's desk. Lee was a chunky, bespectacled man, a little advanced in years for his rank, whose avuncular looks were often at odds with a no-nonsense manner. "Lieutenant Smith," he said, "you're going out to take over MIT #3 at LZ Bayonet. You can turn your duties here over to other people, and be ready to move out the day after tomorrow." Neither he nor Captain Steele bothered to explain why I had earned a coveted command slot right after I had been socked with a severely negative efficiency report, and I didn't ask. I was getting out at last.

As I started packing my gear, I reviewed my chaotically mixed emotions about the sudden, but long-awaited, assignment. True, I was leaving behind the division chickenshit I had been complaining of for so long. And I would no longer have to share living quarters with that horse's ass, Buttroon. And I would be relieved of the gory burden of doing hospital interrogations.

On the other hand, I was being taken out of a heavily fortified division base camp and plunked down in a ragtag pile of bunkers and rusty concertina wire in the middle of Indian country. In terms of distance, the 198th base camp was not far from Americal headquarters, but in terms of safety and comfort it was light-years away. Because it was smaller, farther inland, and defended by fewer men than the division base camp, LZ Bayonet was that much more vulnerable to rocket barrages and close-in mortar fire. It was also easier for the enemy to overrun with a concerted ground attack. During my months at Chu Lai, I had often heard LZ Bayonet down the road getting the shit kicked out of it with mortars and rockets. The night sky over that base camp seemed always to be filled with flares and tracers. In my daily letter to my wife that night, however, I drew an outrageously phony sketch map showing little LZ Bayonet well inside the ring of bunkers, mines and fences protecting the Americal base area. I had my own fears, but I didn't want my wife to share them. When I got home, if I got home, I would tell her the truth.

Still, when I finished reviewing the pros and cons, I wanted to go. It would be my first real chance to command men, a task for which I had been readying myself through four years of ROTC, a year of active duty training, and more than six months in the combat zone. Of course, being an officer had brought certain advantages to being in the army—better pay and living conditions and a measure of self-respect. But the reason I became an officer in the first place was to get the chance to exercise leadership. I had been watching various army officers lead men for over five years, and I had seen a lot of them screw it up. I was sure I could do better, no matter what my lousy OER said. In my head I carried a model, an ideal, of what a competent officer should be, and this was my opportunity to put theory into practice.

Besides, I was well prepared to take command of MIT #3. I had been the acting section chief for the division IPW section; I had conducted innumerable interrogations, and had handled all aspects of document exploitation. I spoke Vietnamese a little better now. I had conducted operations in the field. A brigade intelligence team and its interpreters performed the same functions, only on a smaller scale than at division. I knew how to do every job my men at MIT #3 would be doing, and that personal experience would be invaluable when I supervised them, or so I believed.

In a sense, I had been waiting all my life for this chance. At the 198th Brigade, I would get to apply everything I had learned, in and out of the army, for the remaining months of my time in Vietnam. I was terrified and overjoyed at the same time.

Taking leave of Chu Lai was relatively uncomplicated. Captain Steele had finally figured out that hospital interrogations put too much stress on one person, so he assigned a rotating roster of three enlisted men to the task. I showed my replacements around the hospital and waited while one of them vomited into "my" bush outside the emergency room. I turned the document files over to an IPW lieutenant who had just arrived in country, then said brief good-byes to the few people I cared about: Sergeant Minh, Alvarez, and Larry Hiller, who still had little idea of how to keep track of documents. I even shook hands stiffly with the warrant officer who had refused to accompany me on the Duc Pho convoy. It embarrassed me to think this jerk was the only social friend I had made in base camp.

In the Operational Reports—Lessons Learned documents I later obtained from the Defense Department, it said that 26,500 pages of enemy documents had been processed between October 1968 and January 1969. Add to that the pages I had processed in the months before October, and you have a grand total of 56,500 documents that had passed through my hands since I had arrived the previous July. The detainee totals for October–January (27 North Vietnamese POWs, 37 Viet Cong POWs, 438 CDs, 16 *chieu hoi* volunteers, and 11,458 ICs) showed the enormous number of civilians we had to screen in order to find enemy soldiers. In his report for this period, Captain Steele wrote that the brigade intelligence detachments had been reorganized into MITs of ten to twelve each, and that the teams would be under the operational control of the brigade S-2 (staff intelligence) officers. This meant that, essentially, I was going to be on my own out at LZ Bayonet. The S-2 officer, usually an infantry major with no MI branch training, could assign specific tasks to me and my unit, but he was not officially my commanding officer. My true commanding officer, Captain Steele, would be miles away and in no position to look over my shoulder every minute. This, then, was going to be an independent command for me. Instead of acting out the role of the rebel against authority, as I had all my life, I was going to be the authority, the "Old Man," myself. If that was the case, then who was I going to rebel against? Myself? Psychologically speaking, it would be a novel situation for me.

The night before I left, I stayed awake for a long time wondering about it.

# CHAPTER 18

# LZ Bayonet

I waited a full week before giving my first order.

There were two reasons for this. First, I was new to the business of commanding a unit of my own; the most prudent course was to keep my mouth shut and my eyes open. I could begin to assert myself after I learned how the team functioned and how its various members got along. Second, this was no ordinary unit. The four interrogators, four interpreters and three CI agents, who together with their commanding officer made up MIT #3, were collectively nicknamed the "Dirty Dozen" by other members of the Americal intelligence community. The nickname derived from the popular 1967 movie about a group of neurotic oddballs and misfits recruited from military prisons to undertake a secret mission during World War II. It had been applied to the men of MIT #3 because of their reputation for unruly behavior, disrespect for authority, and general contempt for doing things the army way.

I had seen the guys a few times before at the division MID stand-down parties thrown at Chu Lai every few months for the outlying intelligence teams. Even in a war zone known for weird goings-on, they stood out. They would roll into the IPW compound just as the barbecued meat came off the grill, wolf down their food, drink stupefying amounts of alcohol, remove most of their clothes, and then proceed to offend every superior officer in attendance with obscene gestures and wonderfully creative insults. Invariably, after being told by Captain Steele or the MID commander that they were escaping punishment only because booze had rendered them temporarily insane, the men of MIT #3 would be ordered to leave early. I had also heard a rumor, which the men eventually confirmed for me, that a month earlier, when Lieutenant McDodge had been away on leave, the men took it upon themselves to round up and question every Vietnamese whore along a ten-mile strip of Highway 1. After collecting a couple of truckloads of giggling hookers, the men "interrogated" the women during a two-day marathon of drinking and free fucking. There was talk of an investigation when this story made it back to division, but it was finally dropped because, where the Dirty Dozen was concerned, no one could separate outrageous fact from fiction.

Another story about MIT #3 had made the rounds before I went out there. In late December they had been providing intelligence support for a 198th Brigade sweep operation on the Batangan Peninsula south of Chu Lai. One of the men, Spec Four (specialist, fourth class) Wayne Bingham, had been faced one afternoon with literally hundreds of detainees pulled in during that day's action. Rather than screen through them one at a time (an impossible task, anyway), Bingham impatiently chose to get down to basics—he stood on a folding field table in front of the crowd and, employing his bullhorn and a shocked interpreter, issued the following instructions: "All right, all you dinks, listen up! I want Viet Cong to line up on my left, North Vietnamese troops to line up on my right, and innocent civilians in the center. Now move!" Amazingly, according to the story, all the VC, NVA, and ICs sheepishly sorted themselves into three neat lines in front of Bingham's table. He was then able to dismiss the civilians and concentrate on the true prisoners of war.

This story may have been apocryphal, but it was no exaggeration to say that the Dirty Dozen had become minor legends at MID headquarters. Some of them had been assigned to MIT #3 because of "personality conflicts with superiors" (as their records said), and others had been awarded decorations for valor in the field, but all of them were characters, and none of them, I guessed, would be easy to command.

I was particularly puzzled by the relationship I was expected to establish with the three counterintelligence agents in my new unit. Based on what I had observed at division, the CI operation seemed to function with minimal supervision from anyone outside CI. At Fort Holabird I had learned only the basics about this vaguely shadowy member of the MI family. Its mission was primarily defensive: to protect the army from enemy agents and information-gathering activities, sabotage, and subversion, and to prevent the army from betraying itself through careless talk or mishandling of classified material. CI also kept tabs on all army personnel to make sure none of us became spies for whatever enemies we had around the world, and there were plenty in those days. In this sense, CI was the army's cop, a police organization designed to protect it from internal and external intelligence threats.

At the tactical level—with combat units in Vietnam—CI had to carry out its mission under more trying conditions than usual. Hardly any of the agents I met could speak Vietnamese, yet they were still required to snoop around to find out if the enemy was also snooping around our base camps. Most American camps were flooded with Vietnamese civilians—hootch maids, construction workers, barbers, laundresses, general laborers, and God knows who else—and it was generally assumed that most of them were working for the VC in some capacity. It was part of CI's job to screen these masses of people and somehow find a way to intercept the bad guys, or at least neutralize them. As far as I was concerned, it was an impossible task so long as we lazy Americans allowed the Vietnamese to do our base-camp chores. CI agents were also dispatched to nearby villages and towns to take the pulse, as it were, of people in the territory surrounding our installations. How big, lumbering, obviously Caucasian agents who could barely speak a word of the local language were able to pick up any useful information this way was a mystery to me.

A month or so later, after I had been with MIT #3 for a while, I decided to accompany an agent on one of his day-long jaunts outside LZ Bayonet. I thought it would make me look like a better (braver?) officer to share a bit of the risk one of my men routinely took, and frankly I was curious about how he would go about gathering information out in the boondocks. We drove down to the southern end of the Chu Lai beach, turned right, and continued for several miles along the surf line until we reached the most beautiful village I had ever beheld. I had no idea such a place still existed in that ravaged country. Perched over a blue inlet of the South China Sea was a graceful gathering of thatched huts mounted on tall wooden stilts. The whole picture was framed by palm trees and picturesque fishing boats. I supposed the stilts were to keep the huts dry when the tide rolled in, but the effect was of a little South Sea island paradise cloistered away from the war and even the twentieth century. The CI agent, who wore a regulation jungle fatigue uniform and so was not pretending to be anything but an American soldier, left me in the jeep and wandered seemingly at random around the center of the village. He stopped frequently to chat with various women, children, and old men, using a pidgin of Vietnamese, GI jargon, and hand gestures. Periodically he returned to the jeep to grab a carton of Salem menthol cigarettes from a pile on the back seat. After a few hours he had passed out all the cartons and presumably picked up tidbits of information in exchange. He may also have given the villagers money, but I didn't actually see that.

On the way back to LZ Bayonet late in the afternoon, the agent explained that he had asked the villagers about members of the VC infrastructure who lived in the area, whether any strangers had visited the village recently, and what their attitudes were about Americans. Some had answered him honestly, he thought, some had clearly lied, and others either refused to speak or avoided him altogether. "None of it may be important by itself," he said, "but all of it together gives us a mosaic picture of what's going on near the base camp." That was about all I was ever told about CI operations that were taking place under "my command." Jack Casey, the sergeant who headed the three-man CI detachment as well as functioning as my second in command, would later fend off most of my questions about his activities reminding me that, under army security regulations, I didn't have a "need to know" any more than the little I was being told. I accepted this as yet another example of endemic MI paranoia. I was getting used to it by then.

On the day I arrived at LZ Bayonet, a gala barbecue was in progress at the MIT #3 compound. I learned later that "my" men (they were now mine, for better or worse) had worked a trade with the brigade base camp's mess sergeant. He supplied them with unauthorized steaks to grill, and in return, they let him take a weekly shower in the team's main bathroom. This was a special shower, however, equipped with an electric water heater my men had purchased through a Sears & Roebuck mail-order catalog with their own money. A hot shower anywhere in the Americal Division was such a rarity that it was a valuable bargaining chip in the old army game of trade-offs, or scrounging as we called it.

After dismissing my division driver, I joined the party and took my first look around. The team compound was made up of two long, single-story hootches facing each other across a narrow, dirt parade ground, and various storage huts placed apparently at random around the perimeter. One building was partitioned into six "rooms" for officers and CI noncoms assigned to the team. The larger of the two, this hootch contained the main unit bathroom, which was cleverly equipped with running water fed by gravity from scrounged air force wing tanks mounted on the roof. The mail-order hot shower was in there, too. My room, although smaller than the living space I occupied back at division, was furnished with a comfortable navy bunk and mattress, ample mosquito netting, a folding table, and a crank-activated field telephone. Under the circumstances, it looked quite cozy.

My interrogators all lived together in the barrackslike hootch across the parade ground, and the interpreters, who were still officially part of the ARVN intelligence detachment, bunked in another hootch a short distance away. The POW cage, located about seventy yards across an open space from the central compound, was simply a miniature version of the one at Chu Lai. Our cage and compound had been placed in the northwestern quadrant of the 198th Brigade's main base camp, which itself was set down a quarter mile or so inland of Highway 1. LZ Bayonet wasn't a pretty place by any standard. A few dozen sagging, weather-beaten wood hootches dotted the nondescript coastal landscape, finally petering out at the foot of a line of squat hills to the west. Guard bunkers were placed at wide intervals behind rows of concertina wire strung in a ragged circle around the base camp. It looked like the kind of drab hillbilly hamlet you might find in the less desirable boondocks of the American south. Except for the touches of red, white, and blue on the huge U.S. flag drooping from a flagpole in the main parade ground, all color seemed drained from the scene. Dust or army camouflage coated everything in sight.

The visible prospects may have looked bleak, but not my personal ones. I was at last going to command a unit, however small, and I had a lot to learn.

The men paid little attention to me at first, so I kept to myself for a while. I poked around the compound, inspecting my new home, and carried my gear to my quarters in the main hootch. I ate some of the scrounged steak and started a letter to my wife. "I'm not sure, but I think I'm going to like it here," I wrote. Then I fell asleep on my bunk, wondering vaguely why the men were acting so aloof toward their new commanding officer.

I was awakened late in the afternoon by the familiar sound of chopper blades whirring overhead. They sounded close. "Log birds coming in, sir," one of the men peeked a head in my alcove to say, then disappeared. Remembering that "log birds" meant logistical supply helicopters, I ran out the door and saw a flight of them descending on the little pad next to the POW cage. From their ramps and door bays emerged a flood of Vietnamese—old people, military-age males, children, women clutching bags of belongings, even farm animals. My interrogators and interpreters were directing them to gather at points around the cage and inside the team hootch in the middle of the barbed-wire enclosure. It all looked impossibly chaotic to my eyes, which were accustomed to the rigid order of the Chu Lai cage and the small number of prisoners we received there. But in a short time my men had efficiently separated the obvious ICs (and four-legged creatures) from the milling crowd and begun to interview likely CDs and POWs. The men of my team were obviously used to working without supervision from above, so I stayed out of it and watched them do their jobs.

As quickly as the men were screening their detainees, however, it became clear that they could use some help. Brigade infantry units apparently picked up whole villages full of people on sweep operations, inundating the POW cage with people. Did this indiscriminate dumping happen every evening? Later I found out it did. At division, we generally received only detainees who had already been passed through brigade interrogation points, so until now I had no idea what crowd scenes the brigade teams had to handle on a regular basis. Luckily, interrogations at this early stage were intended only to weed out ICs and obtain information of immediate tactical value to brigade units, so they didn't have to be as comprehensive as the ones we performed at Chu Lai.

Still, it looked like my men would be at it all night, and I wanted to be useful. I walked into the office, threading my way past protesting women and screaming kids, and said to one of the interrogators, "Give me some screening forms and a pen."

"What for, sir?"

"So I can give you guys a hand, that's what for."

He gave me a blank look. "But Lieutenant McDodge didn't do interrogations, sir. He, er, didn't know how to."

"Well, I do. Give me the stuff. Now, when I finish screening each detainee, where do I put the completed form? Over here on the desk?"

The interrogator set me up with what I needed and explained the paper flow. He returned to his own questioning, throwing occasional doubtful glances at me over his shoulder. I was something new to him, an officer who knew how to do the same job he was doing. It wasn't odd to me, of course. At Chu Lai, officers and enlisted men conducted interrogations on an equal basis, and I saw no reason to avoid that at the 198th. If anything, my knowledge of Vietnamese gave me an edge over the enlisted interrogators, many of whom had received little or no language training.

I worked without a break until midnight when the mass interrogation was completed, and fell into bed back in my room. I couldn't imagine Lieutenant McDodge not sharing such an ordeal with his men. Rank had its privileges, of course, but that didn't include goofing off while men under your command busted their asses. This seemed a basic principle of leadership to me, one I had studied as far back as freshman ROTC classes at Georgetown. I didn't think what I had done that night was anything special, but I would find out that, to the men of MIT #3, I had made a good first impression. "Maybe this guy isn't such a screaming asshole, after all" is what I later learned they said to each other in their hootch that night. Maybe they were right.

The next morning, Sp. 4 Wayne Bingham asked me how I was able to sort through so many Vietnamese so quickly and pick out the NVA troopers. I told him that back at division I had acquired the knack of recognizing the slight physical and linguistic differences between North and South Vietnamese men—the northerners tended to be taller, somewhat leaner and with darker complexions and more Chinese-looking features than their southern cousins. And, of course, they spoke with a different accent. One trick I had used the night before was to write a couple of key words on index cards and ask the prisoner to say them out loud. The word *dai*, for instance, was pronounced "yay" by southerners and "zai" by men who had lived above the DMZ all their lives. Northerners generally spoke more harshly and abruptly than southerners, too, which was similar to the situation we had in the United States, where a New Yorker's guttural accent could be distinguished from, say, a South Carolinian's soft drawl. Years later, after I came to live in Annapolis, Maryland, I was introduced to the pretty owner of a Vietnamese restaurant that had just opened in town. She told me everyone called her by her American nickname, but her real name in Vietnamese was Do Thi Trang. For fun, I spoke a few Vietnamese phrases to her, and when she replied, it was in an unmistakable northern accent, the accent of my past enemy. I was taken aback somewhat by this. Old interrogation habits die hard, so I asked where she was from in Vietnam. She told me that her family had lived in Saigon for years before fleeing to America, but before that they had all been raised in Hanoi, in the North. That didn't surprise me a bit.

I spent the rest of my first week at MIT #3 observing,

reading over files, and learning about the brigade my team was serving. The 198th Light Infantry Brigade was composed of three eight-hundred-man maneuver battalions, the 1st Batallion, 6th Infantry (1/6th); the 1st Battalion, 46th Infantry (1/46th); and the 1st Battalion, 52d Infantry(1/52d), as well as various administrative and support units headquartered at LZ Bayonet. The odd-sounding battalion designations, I learned came from U.S. Army history, when units used to be organized into regiments. After the regimental system was abolished in favor of the brigade system, battalions retained their old regimental number as part of the official unit designation. Thus, the 1/52d was actually the 1st Battalion of the old 52d Regiment. The 198th Brigade's tactical area of operations was smaller than those of the Americal's other two brigades, but we were still facing the same dangerous mix of NVA, main force VC, and local force VC. It was also the job of the 198th to protect the main division base camp at Chu Lai from being attacked and overrun.

From my observations of MIT #3, I could see that some changes needed to be made. The most important one was the duty roster. Despite the fact that the team's work was all done at night, after the log birds arrived with that day's load of prisoners, some idiot had decreed that all of the men had to sit in the POW cage office all day. Even though absolutely nothing of significance happened during the daylight hours, my men were being confined unnecessarily to a tiny, unbearably hot hootch just to keep up the appearance of being on duty like everyone else in the base camp. This seemed senseless to me, so I changed it. Before calling my first official meeting with the men, I drew up a rotation list that required only two men to be in the office during the day. The rest were free to do whatever they wanted, so long as they kept me informed of their whereabouts at all times. Each evening, of course, all of them were expected to be present for interrogation duty at the cage. This way most of the men would be fresh for their work, which nearly always called for them to be up until the early hours of the following morning.

The other change I wanted to introduce was volleyball. Back at division I had learned at first hand that a freewheeling, competitive game like this did wonders for relieving stress and building unit morale. And besides, I missed playing.

I called the first team meeting a week after my arrival. I had learned that all of the men were high school graduates and that many had attended at least two years of college. This was unusual for the draftee army America had sent to Vietnam, and it meant that, intellectually, my men were a cut above the norm. I was glad of this because I had no desire to treat them like dumb children. During the past week, I had watched them do a superb job of running the unit almost by themselves, and it was clear they would react negatively to oversupervision. In short, they reminded me of myself—resentful of authority, but more than competent to do the job. Good. Then we were going to get along just fine.

"As you guys already know," I said to the group gathered in the POW cage office, "your nickname is the Dirty Dozen. Now, I could tell you that division sent me down here to straighten you out and make good little soldiers out of you. I could also lie to you and say that I was a perfect little soldier myself at division."

I could see sparks of interest coming into their eyes.

"But that's bullshit. I had some personality conflicts, too, and I suspect that Captain Steele at division IPW sent me down here because he knows we all think alike. None of that matters, though, because I could see this past week that you all are very good at your jobs and you don't need a lot of chickenshit from me. So I'm not going to give you any. If we just continue to do the work here on time, and make sure our interrogation and CI reports get to the people who need them, division isn't going to bother us. And I'm going to make damn sure division doesn't bother you."

Then I issued my first two orders. I told them about my new duty roster, which raised a lot of eyebrows, and I told them that every evening from then on we would hold a team volleyball game before the log birds came in. I would get a net and ball from special services. There was some groaning at that, but I said "Believe me, you're going to love it." And they did.

Late that night, I went through my first mortar attack. I

was standing out in the cage compound talking to one of my men when the first rounds hit a few dozen yards away. By their low-intensity explosions, I could tell they were small 60mm mortars that the VC had scrounged from old French and U.S. stockpiles—dangerous, but nothing like the Soviet 82mm mortars and 140mm rockets I was used to being shelled with at Chu Lai. The little mortars were probably being fired from just over the hills behind the POW cage. Still, from long habit, I broke and ran to the nearest bunker to wait out the attack. I was lying face-down in the bunker when the senior sergeant of the team, Rick Schwartz, crawled in and said respectfully, "Er, Lieutenant Smith, don't you think we better get the prisoners under cover first?"

Shit! I had forgotten all about the fifty or so prisoners we had out in the cage compound. At division I had never been expected to worry about such matters—only my own hide—when the base camp was under fire. I jumped to my feet, embarrassment flushing all over my red face. "Jesus, Rick, you're right. Where's the bunker for the prisoners?"

"You're in it, sir."

I had to laugh, and so did he. We ran outside and gathered all the prisoners into the bunker to await the end of the attack. I still had a lot to learn.

# CHAPTER 19

# The Old Man

The first challenge to my untested authority over MIT #3 came from above rather than below. When word got around the base camp that I was giving my men "vacations" from duty at the POW cage office, I began to get visitors at the compound—first a captain from the brigade TOC, then a major from the S-2 section, and finally the burly colonel who commanded the 198th Brigade. Each had pretty much the same message to convey. "Who the hell do you think you are giving men time off in a combat zone? This is an outrage and a threat to military discipline. Those men will run wild. Return them to full duty immediately!"

My reply to each of them was the same, too. "I will run my unit as I see fit. It's stupid to keep men frying in a hootch all day when their real work is at night. I trust them not to abuse their freedom, and if you don't like it, go fuck yourself." I never used exactly those words, of course. Disrespect to a superior officer was forbidden under all circumstances. Nevertheless, I made it clear that, although they might outrank me, they could not give either me or any of my men a direct order. My understanding was that MIT #3 was an "attached" unit, one that could be given tasks to do by brigade authorities but which could not be commanded by anyone but me or my own superior back at division. And that was that. I invited the captain, the major, and the colonel to contact Captain Steele back at Chu Lai if they had a problem, but meanwhile I had a job to do.

Once out of their presence, I shook in my jungle boots, of course. Lieutenants weren't supposed to oppose senior

officers like that, even if lieutenants believed they were
right. But at division, I had been tyrannized by so many
petty army dictators and been forced to eat so much
chickenshit that I decided to chance the wrath of Captain
Steele when he found out about my stand. I also felt that if
I was going to become a true commanding officer, and not
just a message-bearer from above, I needed to establish my
independence right off. I also wanted to protect my men
from interference from above. I expected to get an angry
call from Captain Steele at any minute, but surprisingly
none came. A week or two later, when I called him to
make a routine report, he mentioned casually that he had
been contacted by "some upset people" at my brigade. He
told them, he said, that he trusted my judgment in such
matters and that if they still had a problem to take it up
with me.

Whew!

From that moment on, I detected a different tone in
Steele's manner toward me. I also began to see him in a
more favorable light. Was it possible that our unpleasant,
incessantly adversarial relationship was going to change for
the better? At the time, I thought it was too much to hope
for, but time fooled me in the end. The men of MIT #3
didn't fool me, though. For my entire tenure at the team,
they never once did anything wild or improper during their
off-duty periods (most of the time they slept, in fact), and
only once did any of them leave the base camp without telling me.

With the matter of work schedules out of the way, at
least for a while, I turned my attention to other duties I had
never encountered as a staff officer at division. Virtually
everything that happened at MIT #3 concerned me—getting
water shipments for the bathroom wing tanks; settling
disputes among the men; keeping the interpreters happy; ar-
ranging for resupply of pencils, paper clips, and interrogation forms; making sure the unit jeeps were in working
order; surveying, maintaining, and doling out all the miscellaneous equipment assigned to the unit, including jeep trail-
ers, gas masks, C rations, ammunition, tents, office
furniture, and even a fifteen-foot Boston Whaler (with out-

board motor) my everscrounging men had somehow acquired as surplus from the army transportation corps.

The jeeps, as always, were a problem. We had two assigned to MIT #3, and they never seemed to be functional at the same time. If something went wrong with a vehicle, the official procedure was to arrange to have it towed to the brigade motor pool and repaired in due course. Unofficially, of course, it seldom worked that way. This was Vietnam, after all, the Bermuda Triangle for army rules. My second-in-command, a twenty-seven-year-old CI sergeant named Jack Casey, informed me during my second week that motor pool repairs took weeks and sometimes even months. "It's total bullshit, Lieutenant Smith. If you want our jeeps to get fixed, you've got to take matters into your own hands."

"What do you mean by that, Jack?"

"Well, I know how to do a little mechanical stuff. I can fix most of the crap that goes wrong with the jeeps if I can just get my hands on the parts. If you catch my meaning?"

I still didn't understand. Jack, who was only four years older than I, nevertheless, had taken a fatherly approach to me as soon as we met. He was a "lifer" who planned to make the army a career and who was already an experienced noncom in direct charge of the CI agents assigned to my team. It was traditional for senior sergeants to bring green young lieutenants under their wings, but even though I wasn't so green at that point and Jack wasn't all that senior, we fell comfortably into the traditional mold. Now he was trying to tell me that unorthodox methods were necessary to keep our jeeps on the road, and the opportunity to use them came up just a couple of days after our conversation.

"Now look, here's what we're going to do," he said after reporting that one of the jeeps had conked out and needed a new carburetor. As instructed, I went back to my hootch to change into my newest-looking set of fatigues and to demote myself by pinning one of my old second-lieutenant's gold bars on my cap. We drove in the remaining jeep over to the motor pool, and Jack let me off at the entrance to the main office. Behind this wooden building lay a vast motor park full of vehicles, some of which were so new they had never even been assigned to a unit. Jack told me that during the day, the few guards on duty tended to loiter inside the office. While Jack drove to the back end of the motor park, I stalked into the office, screeching in an artificially high voice, "I demand to see the man in charge here! I can't get any jeeps fixed, and I want to know why!"

I stayed there, distracting the clerks, mechanics, and guards by playing the role of a petulant, spoiled young lieutenant who wanted action *now*, damn it, while Jack quietly jumped the motor park fence and expertly lifted a carburetor from one of the brand-new jeeps. He appeared in the office a short time later, saying, "Look, guys, Lieutenant Smith is new in country. He doesn't know how things work yet. C'mon, sir, let's go, okay?" I let him escort me out the door, while I waved my arms around and protested that "My father is a general in Washington, you know, and I'm going to tell him what lousy motor pools we have in Vietnam!" Laughing at the success of our little ruse, Jack and I drove back to the POW compound, with our booty under a canvas cover. That afternoon, he replaced the old jeep carburetor with the new one, and all was well with MIT #3 for a while. This incident taught me that I was apparently willing to do anything necessary to take care of the needs of my new command, including making an utter fool of myself.

My feelings of protectiveness toward the men grew stronger each day, and it was largely because I was beginning to realize that I had the power of life and death over them. This aspect of the job of command had never occurred to me before, and it was not a pleasant duty. The interrogators and interpreters under my care were safe enough while they were screening prisoners at the cage inside the base camp, of course. Except for occasional rocket and mortar barrages and a few sniper rounds fired from outside the perimeter, life at LZ Bayonet seemed to be relatively uneventful. But part of the mission of MIT #3 was to provide interrogation teams to our maneuver elements (the three infantry battalions) in the field. That meant that I had to dispatch my men outside the base camp whenever they were requested by company commanders and platoon leaders operating in our tactical zone. These requests came regularly, two or three times a week, and I assigned each interrogator-interpreter team on the basis of a rotating roster—if your name was next on the list, you went out on the next field mission.

When the first request came in, though, I wasn't mentally prepared for it. I was playing a pickup game of poker with the men in their hootch one night, trying to keep my mind on the game despite the sounds of explosions in the distance. The VC were apparently pounding away with mortars on poor LZ Gator, a battalion fire support base a few miles down Highway 1 from our camp, and our forces were replying with artillery and helicopter gunships. The men around the poker table showed no concern, however, presumably because that was LZ Gator's problem, not ours. Through the hootch window I saw brilliant flashes of acid phosphorescent light from flares, and deeper oranges thrown against the black horizon from the impacts of high-explosive shells. The electrically rotated barrels of miniguns mounted on our helicopters and C-130 gunships (ironically nicknamed Puff the Magic Dragon, after the gentle folk song by Peter, Paul and Mary) churned out thousands of rounds per minute into the dark ground beyond LZ Gator's bunker line. A prolonged burst of tracer bullets from a minigun sounded like a sick baby spitting food.

The game went on until we were interrupted by the bell on the field telephone I had brought over and rigged beside the table (I had to be "on call" at all times). The brigade TOC was calling to pass on a priority request from LZ Gator to send an interrogation team. Grunts on the bunker line down there had captured a couple of enemy sappers and wanted information out of them pronto. This meant that I'd have to put one of my teams on a chopper to be inserted into LZ Gator while it was still under attack, a nasty proposition. The next name on my mission roster was Rick Schwartz, the senior interrogator of the team and a man who had already collected two Purple Hearts for wounds in combat. Technically he was supposed to be my second-in-command, but he had asked me to relieve him of that duty because he was reluctant to oversee men he had been working with so closely for almost a year. I honored his request and picked Jack Casey for the slot instead; Jack was senior to Schwartz anyway, and better suited, I thought, to assist me in running the team.

As soon as I told Rick Schwartz he was tapped for the LZ Gator mission, he folded his hand and walked over to his bunk to pack his combat gear. He might be away for a day or more. To my amazement, because I had never witnessed this ritual before, the rest of the men left the table and gathered around Schwartz.

"Hey, Rick," one of them said, "if you get your legs blown off down at Gator, can I have your extra pair of jungle boots?"

"Sure, man, you can have my poncho, too."

"Rick, old buddy," another one said, "you ain't gonna need that wooden box you keep your stereo in if you die and go to heaven, right? Can I have it then?"

"Yep, but make sure my beer can collection goes to Alvarez back at division. I promised him he'd get it if I got zapped."

It took me a while to realize I was watching an impromptu "last will and testament" that Schwartz was making to his friends. The group's almost sacrilegious bantering and wisecracking about death was, I later figured out, a way of coping with the immediacy of the possibility of death on any given day, or in this case, night. By talking so openly about the worst, maybe the worst wouldn't happen this time. Over the next months, I witnessed that farewell rite many times, but like many things I saw in Vietnam, I never quite got used to it. Simply and brutally put, these men could have their lives taken away because of orders I gave. That night, I strengthened my resolve to protect them as much as possible for as long as I commanded them. Suddenly all my years of training to accomplish the mission and all the talk I used to hear back at Fort Benning about "winning the war" seemed like pure, unrefined bullshit. I no longer cared about what the army wanted me to do, only about the men the army had put in my hands. If that wasn't a "professional" attitude, if it was a treasonous thought to put my men ahead of the mission, I didn't give a flying, foaming fuck. If I could prevent it, nobody was going to die on my watch.

Rick Schwartz came back from LZ Gator late the next

day, fortunately, none the worse for wear. An infantry lieutenant had tried to keep him there for another night, just in case a second attack took place, but Schwartz managed to rebuff him. I had been noticing since I arrived that my men frequently experienced trouble getting back out of the field. Once I even had to get on the TOC radio to a platoon leader and demand that he return my interrogation team or else I was going to fly out and retrieve the men myself. As soon as they had an interrogation team on the spot, many field commanders were reluctant to give up the ability to question the prisoners they picked up. Since all of my men held the enlisted ranks of specialist fourth class (paygrade E-4) or sergeant (E-5), they found it difficult to refuse officers' requests (and sometimes orders) to remain with infantry units in the field. Staying out there, especially at night, was how men got killed, however, and my interrogators were not grunts. Their job was to assist fighting units with a specific task—questioning prisoners—not to do the fighting themselves. Furthermore, my men, like MIT #3 itself, were attached to field units, not under the direct command of their officers. If an officer kept one of my men beyond the scheduled time, he was usurping my authority and, more importantly, endangering my men.

I thought about this problem for a while, and then got in my jeep and drove to the main PX back at Chu Lai. As an officer I was supposed to rate my own driver, but I felt uncomfortable wasting anyone's time with a task I could perform perfectly well myself, so I went alone. There I bought several sets of gold second-lieutenant's bars and drove back with them. I called the men together and said, "Look, I'm going to give you these bars to wear when you go into the field. You will not—I repeat, not—give anyone orders or act in any way like you are an officer. You will keep your mouths shut and do your jobs like always. But if any grunt officer, especially a lieutenant, tries to give you shit about staying in the field past the time you think is necessary, these bars will give you the clout to refuse. Officers will be less likely to fuck with you if they think you're officers, too. Is that all understood? Okay, now take the bars and put them on only after you leave on a mission."

Was my action unconventional? Yes. Was it against strict

army regulations? Absolutely. Was I taking a chance that my men would abuse the privilege? Yes. Did I give a shit about any of that? Nope. I was trying to protect them, and that was all I really cared about. I knew I was acting like a fretting mother hen, but it didn't bother me much. If my fellow officers in the field were abusing their rank by detaining my men without authorization from me, then I was going to fight abuse with my own brand of abuse. In fact, there were never any problems. As I expected, I could trust the men to carry out my instructions without violating the limits I set. And that was one less worry I had on my mind on nights when my men were out in the field. Even mother hens have to sleep sometime.

Those first few weeks at LZ Bayonet were incredibly busy, confusing, frightening at times, and more thoroughly satisfying than any period I had so far spent in country. At last, I was getting to run my own show and run it my way. As I had hoped when I heard I might be given the assignment, I was finally able to put all my training and experience to work. A letter to my wife late in February gives some idea of the variety and the frenetic pace of my new duties:

> This can't be too long a letter, honey, as this hectic day, already three-fourths over, hasn't even really begun My problems as CO [actually I was just an officer-in-charge—OIC—but I was trying to impress my wife with the more imperial-sounding title of commanding officer. I doubt she knew the difference or cared] do not necessarily remain limited to the production of intelligence for the brigade. Today, for instance, I staved off an administrative attempt by those assholes at division to transfer all of my CI people (including Jack Casey) back up to division. To do it I had to make 6 telephone calls, write a 'position paper' explaining why I needed to keep them, and then make visits to three brigade S-2 officers and two division MID officers to argue my case. It worked, however.
>
> Then I had a knock-down, drag-out argument with the captain who runs the unit that gives us rations and sleeping quarters. The argument was about his not wanting

my "dinks" (my ARVN interpreters) to eat in "his" mess hall. I finally had to get the MID commander, the executive officer, and the assistant brigade commander to squash this mad, dink-hating captain - especially since my interpreters threatened to quit unless they could eat in the mess hall.

All this was in addition to writing two rating forms, four PW reports, conducting a liaison visit of ARVN headquarters here at the 198th, holding two section meetings and getting my Asian Flu shot (ironic touch, that)! AND ... it's 4:00 pm - in one hour we have two chopper-loads of detainees coming in, including assorted VC, one ARVN deserter, and a homicidal prostitute from An Tan coming in for interrogation. That means, in addition to a full night's work, two briefings I have to conduct tonight on the results of our interrogations, and one more tomorrow at 5:30. The shit is really flying today. I love you. More later.

Another of my unusual collateral duties as commander of MIT #3 was to supervise, and sometimes participate in, the constant scrounging and trading my men engaged in to keep the unit running. One of the most sought-after commodities in Vietnam in the winter of 1969 was plywood, and it was traded so often for other items that it became an unofficial medium of exchange among the troops. I never understood completely why sheets of plywood were so important to everyone, but I did notice that my men used them to section off private sleeping quarters for themselves in their barracks. And every hootch in Vietnam, as far as I could see, was constructed of plywood walls, floors, and roofing, so it may not have been so unusual for this ubiquitous, valuable material to be hoarded and used as "money," after all.

When Jack Casey told me we needed a new set of tires for one of our jeeps, for instance, I immediately set in motion the following series of transactions: we traded ten sheets from our stock of plywood to the nearest helicopter squadron in exchange for several Viet Cong flags their pilots had picked up in the field; we bartered the flags and two days of hot shower privileges to the brigade mess sergeant, who gave us a large box of frozen steaks, which we then, in turn, traded to a contact at the motor pool in return for the tires we needed. I was of course appalled that we were forced to become black marketeers just to obtain supplies that officially should have been issued to us as a matter of course, but if the army couldn't meet our needs, we had no choice except to resort to the trusty plywood system.

Just when I thought I was settling in and getting used to life in a brigade base camp, something happened to remind me that I should never stop expecting surprises.

At about noon on a bright, cloudless day, I was walking from my hootch over to the POW cage for a routine visit when my nose began to run violently. Then my eyes suddenly watered up, blinding me temporarily. The skin on my arms, face, and neck was itching, then burning painfully. In a few seconds, I realized I had stepped into the midst of an invisible cloud of gas. The symptoms, which I had experienced during an unforgettable training session back at Fort Benning, told me that I was breathing in CS, a particularly virulent brand of tear gas. At Benning, we had been fitted with gas masks and ordered into a chamber filled with clear clouds of invisible CS. Inside, we were required to rip off our masks and try to repeat our name and serial number to an instructor (who was well protected inside his own gas mask and chemical warfare suit). None of us, of course, was able to get past the first syllables of our names before we were gasping and groping for the nearest exit. Many threw up outside the chamber. It was a lesson we were expected to remember, and it certainly jumped back into my mind as I stumbled around that day at LZ Bayonet.

My first coherent thought was to find my gas mask, which I knew was stored under my bunk. Pressing a handkerchief to my raw, leaking nose, I sprinted back to my hootch, pulled out the gas mask and strapped it onto my face. When I arrived at the Americal, I had been issued a mask and told to keep it handy, even though the chances of getting gassed by our ill-equipped enemy were slim. It was also suggested that I check the mask at least once a month to make sure its face seals were adjusted for tightness and the filter was functioning. For some reason, I had always followed these instructions to the letter, even though I often felt silly taking precautions against a threat so unlikely to materialize.

But now here it was, a cloud of painful, debilitating CS tear gas floating over my base camp. I had no idea where it was coming from, and I began to wonder if it was a preliminary to a VC ground attack. When my eyes and nose cleared up a little inside the safety of my mask, I grabbed my carbine and ran outside to see if enemy soldiers were even then storming over the wire to overrun LZ Bayonet. It came to me that I might be the only one on his feet to oppose the attack, a depressing possibility. All was quiet, however, except for the two dozen or so men within my field of vision who were bent over, coughing and choking from the effects of the gas. In a few minutes the cloud seemed to disperse with the slight breeze that was blowing, and the men began to recover. There were no VC or NVA in sight, thank God.

Later that day, I asked around at the brigade operations center to find out what had happened. No one was precisely sure, but it appeared that one of the CS gas grenades we employed against VC tunnel complexes had fallen into the hands of the enemy, and the best guess was that some VC infiltrator had detonated the grenade somewhere on LZ Bayonet to give us a nasty taste of our own weapon. No one had reported seeing such an infiltrator, and no one had heard an explosion of any kind, but this was the only explanation for the unexpected cloud of gas that had passed through the base camp.

Just before the volleyball game that evening, I told the assembled team that from then on every man would check his gas mask on schedule and keep it close by. Some of them had been caught in the noxious cloud that afternoon, so there wasn't as much grumbling as I had anticipated. I never needed my gas mask again, but I had learned once again that in war I should always expect the unexpected.

# CHAPTER 20

# Twenty-four Hours

By the end of my first month at MIT #3, I realized that a commander's work, like a woman's, is never done. I was far busier than I had ever been at division, and in fact, I was beginning to relish the hectic schedule I kept. Nearly all of the team's interrogations were conducted late in the evening, after everyone at LZ Bayonet but the bunker guards and duty officers had gone to bed, and unforeseen problems of one kind or another continued to crop up at all hours of the day and night.

At about two o'clock one morning, for instance, Jack Casey shook me awake and told me he was worried about his two CI agents. He waited for me to splash water on my face from the five-gallon can I kept beside my bunk and said, "My men haven't come back from An Tan yet. I think you and I ought to go find them."

"What are they doing in the village, Jack? Are they on a mission or something?"

"Shit, no. Those fuckers are partyin'." His Arkansas drawl always thickened under stress. "They got some kind of arrangement with some whores down there, so I figure they're at the whorehouse right now, drunk as hell. They probably forgot they told me they'd be back at midnight or before."

"Okay, let's go look for them. But give me a minute first, Jack. Get the jeep started and pull it up front—and wear full combat gear."

I wasn't used to this kind of request coming in the middle of the night. Back at Chu Lai, I would have been fast

164

asleep under the mosquito netting on my bunk by now, with only an occasional rocket attack to disturb my pleasant dreams of going home. I was also a little confused. Should I report the men missing, as I was sure regulations required, or just go galloping off with Jack to retrieve them? What if they had been captured by the VC, who, from all accounts, enjoyed the whores of An Tan as much as we did? I decided to cover my ass by cranking up my field telephone and calling Captain Steele back at the IPW section for advice, even though he wouldn't appreciate being awakened at that hour any more than I did. After I summarized the situation for him, his reply was unexpectedly vague. "Since I'm not on the spot, Smith, and you are, I cannot officially approve or disapprove of any action you plan on taking. So as far as I'm concerned, I never received this phone call—and you never made it. Have you got that?"

"Yes, sir, I got it," I managed to fit in just before he broke the connection. What he was really saying was that I was the boss and had to accept the consequences of whatever decision I made. This was a different Captain Steele from the controlling nitpicker I knew when I was at Chu Lai, but maybe he suspected that I was becoming a different Lieutenant Smith, too. I climbed into a set of fatigues, put on my boots and pistol holster, grabbed my helmet and flak vest, and ran out the hootch door. I was going to An Tan.

Outside, however, I saw that Jack and I had company. Somehow the rest of the team had heard about the missing agents (the unit grapevine was faster and more accurate than any intelligence we ever gathered) and made a collective decision to accompany us to the village. Seven of them were cramped into the jeep wearing full combat gear. "We thought you could use some help, sir," a grinning Rick Schwartz said as I squeezed myself into the front seat.

One of the unspoken benefits of being in the intelligence branch was that you could legally flaunt a lot of army rules. I knew that LZ Bayonet, like the rest of the Americal's base camps, was under an after-midnight curfew for all personnel, but I also knew we could drive out the main gate with impunity once I identified us to the guard. Because of MI's classified and rather wide-ranging mission in Vietnam, no one ever knew for sure what we could or couldn't do, and I certainly wasn't going to enlighten anybody. After a word with the cowed and cooperative guard, we sped through the darkness north on Highway 1 to An Tan. Jack directed us to the whorehouse he thought his agents were in, a typically ramshackle wood-and-corrugated-sheet-metal structure set back from the muddy main roadway.

I split the team into two groups and told them to fan out on either side of the whorehouse entrance. "Stay out of sight," I called out softly, "and lock and load your weapons." I heard music playing inside, as well as drunken laughter. It all sounded innocent enough, but in an isolated Vietnamese village late at night, I didn't want to take any chances. Jack and I pushed the door open and entered with pistols in hand, but we needn't have worried. The two CI men were lounging on a battered couch with prostitutes on their laps, waving cans of beer around and singing rock-and-roll songs off-key. "Hiya, Lieutenant Smith! Hiya, Jack! Join the party!" one of them said through his alcoholic haze.

We slid their boots on and lugged them to the door. I presumed Jack would deal with them later, as I had no intention of imposing punishment on men under his direct orders. Just outside, however, I saw another jeep parked next to ours. The letters QC were stenciled on the hood, so I knew it belonged to the ARVN military police. A group of them stood by the jeep with carbines in their hands. Their officer stepped forward with a hand up and said, in halting English, "Stop. We take these men under arrest."

In my own halting Vietnamese, I identified myself and asked why. "Whores call us. They say soldiers drunk and yell a lot. We take them in," he said in the authoritative tone cops everywhere have been using for centuries.

"Look, these are my men. I will take them back to the base camp, okay? You can't have them."

The officer produced a huge scowl on his face when I challenged his authority like that. He snapped an order to the policemen behind him, and they raised their weapons. "We take now."

This was why we were losing the war, I thought in disgust. "Allies" of the kind that we and the ARVNs supposedly were should be hunting down the enemy instead of facing off with each other over possession of a pair of drunks. "No take," I said to the officer in Vietnamese, and then in a louder voice in English, "Okay, guys, show yourselves." My men, who had heard the entire exchange, emerged from the shadows beyond the ring of the QC jeep highlights. They stood in a wide semicircle behind the goggle-eyed ARVN policemen with their own weapons raised.

I smiled at the officer to end the stalemate. "I take. I punish. Whores be happy, okay? Thank you," I said. "Get in the jeep," I told Jack and the CI agents. "We go now," I said to the officer. As I backed the jeep away from the front of the whorehouse, I directed Rick Schwartz to withdraw the team on foot, matching my pace and keeping their weapons pointed at the ARVNs. After fifty yards of this careful retreat, everyone jumped into the jeep, and I drove us out of An Tan at top speed.

An hour or so later, after standing by while Jack delivered the classic you-assholes-are-in-big-trouble lecture to his sheepish and now sober agents, I went back to bed. I tried not to think of what would have happened if the entire team hadn't come with Jack and me to An Tan.

And that was only the beginning of a long day.

At 8:00 A.M. the next morning, the bell of the field telephone next to my bunk sounded like it was exploding in my ear. My eyes were gummy, and my stomach was lurching after only a few hours of sleep. It was Major Kanka, the S-2 intelligence officer at the brigade TOC. He was a prune-faced man who made no secret about his intense dislike of the fact that I was not under his direct command.

"I want a report on last night's prisoners, Lieutenant Smith."

"Sir, there isn't much to report. We had a normal batch of detainees with no information of importance." Kanka knew that I would have alerted him long before this if we had turned up anything out of the ordinary. Wake-up calls like these were his way of getting revenge on me for being out of his control loop. I of course didn't tell him about last night's trip to An Tan.

"Nevertheless, I want to see your POW summaries now.

Right now. Don't tell me you were asleep, Smith. At this late hour? There's a war on, you know," he said sarcastically. Major Kanka refused to acknowledge that MIT #3 worked while he and the rest of the TOC staff slept, and he always pretended surprise when he found me groggy after being up late. Right then, however, I didn't feel like dealing with his sneers.

"Hell no, Major. I've been up for hours," I lied.

"Well then, that means you can come right over to the TOC and give me your report in person. I'll expect you in ten minutes."

Shit. I leaped out of bed and stumbled down to the bathroom. No time to shave carefully. Rub cold water in my eyes. Scrape razor over my face. Sprint back to room. Pull on fatigue pants and blouse. Put on boots without socks. Strap pistol holster on. Run to jeep. Pedal to the floor and, bingo! I'm pulling up behind the TOC looking like the living dead. Back at Georgetown University I used to routinely make it to early classes in about the same condition.

Kanka looked me over ruefully when I arrived (in under ten minutes), although he couldn't deny that I was shaved, in uniform, and on my feet, however shakily. I gave him a verbal summary of the trivial POW information from the night before and left with a jaunty salute. Someday I would have the courage to tell that bastard that I had a right to sleep in after a long night in interrogations (not to mention an extra trip to An Tan), but that wasn't going to be the day.

I figured that since I was up and relatively awake anyway, I would catch up on some work at the POW cage. Intending to reinterrogate a detainee who sounded interesting the night before, I stopped at the interpreter's hootch to pick up Sergeant Bo, who had the best command of English in the group. The other interpreters were sleeping, but Bo's bunk was empty. "Bo has gone to Quang Ngai City to see his girlfriend," one of the interpreters told me when I shook him awake. I sat on his bunk, gripped the area just above his bicep and leaned so close to his face I knew he could smell my bad breath from a semisleepless night; I said, "Tell me exactly *where* in Quang Ngai. Give me the address and the girl's name." Under protest, because he didn't want to tattle on a fellow ARVN, he nevertheless gave me the information, including directions to the girl's house in the provincial capital.

My next stop was at the hootch that housed the commander of the ARVN detachment at the 198th Brigade, a skinny captain who barely spoke English. He merely shrugged when I reported Bo's absence without leave. "I can do nothing, *toi sin loi* [sorry]." This was absurd. A soldier waltzes off in the middle of a war without a word to anyone and this maddeningly phlegmatic captain, who was officially his commanding officer, shows no concern whatsoever.

"Well, Captain, do you at least have any idea when Sergeant Bo is coming back?"

He gave me a lopsided grin and another shrug. "*Khong biet* [I don't know]."

It was clear I was wasting my time and breath. I should have known by that late point in my tour that ARVN military discipline often ranged between nonexistent and criminally lax, but I had never encountered such a blatant example of it before. Sergeant Bo was still an interpreter assigned to MIT #3, however, and that made him my problem, too. I had a feeling that I was being tested here. I hadn't been in command very long, and Bo might have mistaken my easygoing attitude for laziness or negligence. If I let him disappear without even the courtesy of telling me, not to mention his own ARVN commander, I could easily lose face with the other interpreters and then face a growing discipline problem of my own. I could expect no help from the ARVN authorities, though.

So it looked like I would have to go and get Bo myself.

I remembered that the MPs assigned to the brigade cage sent a truck full of CD detainees down to a collection camp on the outskirts of Quang Ngai nearly every day, and I knew my own jeeps were already scheduled for others to use that morning. So I arranged with the MP driver to let me hitch a ride on his three-quarter-ton truck, which would be leaving momentarily. He was glad of the company as well as an extra person to keep an eye on the dozen or so prisoners he and only two guards were transporting down Highway 1 to Quang Ngai. The driver also agreed to make a stopover at the girlfriend's house and, after I retrieved Bo (with MP help if necessary), to give us a lift back to LZ Bayonet. I ran back to my hootch for my helmet, pistol, and carbine and met the truck at the main gate. Sergeant Bo was due for a surprise lunch guest.

About ten miles down Highway 1 from LZ Bayonet, the paved surface gave way to dirt, and the driver slowed down to accommodate the potholes and old shell craters pitting the road. We were in open country, riding past rice paddies leading to a village up ahead, when I heard a single gunshot which seemed to have come from an abandoned church fifty or sixty yards to our right. The left front tire burst apart with a flatulent pop, and the truck slewed to a dusty halt in the middle of the road. It was probably a local-yokel VC rifleman taking a lucky potshot, which was not unusual along this unsecured stretch of Highway 1, nicknamed "Sniper Alley" by the troops who traveled it often. We piled out of the truck with weapons at the ready, but the sniper must have faded back into the rice fields because there was no more firing from that quarter.

As I was the senior man present, I suggested that the two guards change the tire while the driver and I walked a perimeter guard around the truck, just in case. We were far from any help in a disabled vehicle, and I was nervous as I paced up and down the pockmarked road with my carbine clutched in my hands. "Hurry up with that tire," I called several times to the sweating guards. Luckily the MPs had thought to bring a spare. A couple of dirty-faced kids from the village nearby wandered up the road to see what was happening, and at first, I paid little attention to them. When one of the prisoners tied up in the back of the truck started talking in a low voice to the kids, however, my ears pricked up. I understood just enough Vietnamese to know he was telling them to get help. He was instructing the kids to run to the VC chief in their village and ask him to come back with troops to free the prisoners. "There are only four Americans," he said, "it will be easy to take them out."

The kids bolted, scrambling up the road to their village less than a quarter mile distant, and suddenly I had a horrible choice to make—if I let the kids go, there was a good chance they'd bring an enemy unit back with them, but if

I wanted to stop them, I'd have to shoot them. Swearing and fumbling with the bolt of my carbine, I chased the kids up the road, shouting, "Halt or I'll shoot!" or something trite like that, but they kept running. I stopped and brought the carbine to my shoulder. My steel front sight blade settled on the fleeing back of the kid closest to me, about twenty yards away, and I had only to squeeze the trigger to blow the child away. "Fuck this!" I yelled to no one in particular and lowered the barrel a few inches. I let off two quick rounds, which kicked plumes of dust up just behind the kid, and he stopped. Hearing the reports, his companion stopped running, too. Thank God.

I grabbed the kids by their hair and roughly hauled them back to the truck. I tied their hands and threw them in the back with the prisoners. We would let them go as we passed through the village, too late for them to alert the local VC. I don't really know if I could have shot them, even to save our lives, but I will be forever grateful that I never had to find out. In twenty minutes the MP guards had changed the tire, and we were back on the road to Quang Ngai.

Once we had delivered our prisoners to the collection camp, we drove slowly into the middle of town with me asking directions along the way. A very pretty young girl wearing a pink *ao dai* pointed out the tiny house where Bo's girlfriend lived. I told the MP driver to leave our truck parked at the east end of the block. I stationed him at the front of the house and the two guards behind it. "If Sergeant Bo tries to get away, don't shoot him, just collar him," I said to the MPs. Then I strode up the front walk and, without knocking, entered.

The front room was empty, but I heard noises coming through the beaded curtain that served as the door to a back bedroom. Pushing through the strings of rattling beads, I saw the back of Bo's naked body lying on top of what I assumed was his girlfriend. His rear end was pumping up and down, and the girl was making ecstatic little cries. Aw, Jesus, I thought, he was humping her, and I had to walk in at precisely the most embarrassing moment for all of us. Instinctively I backed out the door, averting my head as I went. But then I remembered why I was there, returned to the bedroom, and pulled a glassy-eyed, sweat-soaked Bo off the girl. "Look, miss, I'm sorry, but I need him more than you do," I said over my shoulder as I hustled Bo through the beads.

I gave the surprisingly subdued Bo time to dress and kiss his girlfriend (who stared malevolently at me the whole time) good-bye. Then I put him in the truck, and we drove back to LZ Bayonet in silence. Bo made no protests and no excuses, and I gave him no lectures. My actions, I hoped, proved that I had no patience with AWOL interpreters. When I let him off at his hootch, I said, "I understand that you have been fighting for a long time and need to have a life outside the army. Just tell me the next time you need some time off. Maybe we can make some proper arrangements." As it turned out, I never had any problems like that again. As long as the interpreters gave me advance notice of their intent to go "AWOL" for a prearranged period, which they did faithfully from then on, I was able to schedule missions and interrogations around them until they returned, which they always did on time. Otherwise, they knew I would go after them.

It was only midafternoon then, and except for a couple of catnaps, I had been going at full throttle since early the day before. But it wasn't over yet.

Back at the cage, one of the interrogators on duty had good news. "You remember those two dinks we got in last night from the 1/52d, sir? Well, I talked to them again this morning, and they finally coughed up the name or their unit."

This was indeed a welcome development. One of our maneuver battalions, the 1/52d Infantry, had been in heavy contact all the day before with an unknown enemy unit, probably main force VC. Not knowing the name or numerical designation of the unit however, forced the battalion to fight blind. Our men had no idea how many enemy soldiers they were facing, what their weapons were or how stubbornly they would defend themselves. This kind of information could only come from an order-of-battle book, but the book was useless without the name of the unit as a reference. The two prisoners sent in late the previous day from the 1/52d battle area had resisted all our efforts to pry any information out of them. Today, however, they had been convinced to tell us after an extended interrogation.

This was why I had always wanted to be assigned to a brigade intelligence team. Information we extracted from prisoners at the division level was useful on a higher strategic level, of course, but rarely in a fast-moving tactical emergency like this. I was going to be able to help that battalion commander right now, only hours after he had given us prisoners to work with. This, to me, was what combat intelligence was about—getting information fast and giving it right back to the troops who could use it immediately. The interrogator and I looked up the VC unit in our OB files, and I copied down what I thought were the most relevant facts and conclusions. Then I drove over to the TOC and asked for a radio link to the 1/52d Battalion commander in the field. When I told him exactly who he was fighting, how they were armed and equipped, how numerous they were, and based on the unit's history in the OB book, how they were likely to conduct operations against him, he was almost pathetically grateful. I felt like I had given a starving man food, and it felt good.

By early evening, large flocks of log birds were returning to roost. The remainder of that day's battle by the 1/52d had produced more chopper-loads of prisoners, so it was time to end the volleyball game and get to work. At about 12:30 A.M. we finished screening all the prisoners but one. He was a junior VC lieutenant, and because we seldom captured officers, he was the focus of my attention. As I've mentioned before, the run-of-the-mill enemy soldier, VC or NVA, was maddeningly ignorant and uninformed. Most of them knew their own name and how much of a rice ration they would receive each week (if they were lucky) and not much else. Officers could read a map, at least, and be helpful in a lot of ways. If they were handled correctly, of course.

There was only one man in the team I trusted to interrogate such a prize catch, and that was Rick Schwartz. Although he had received virtually no language training that I knew of, Rick had somehow managed to acquire a fair fluency in Vietnamese, possibly from his long-time girlfriend in one of the nearby villages. More importantly, he seemed to understand instinctively how the Vietnamese mind worked and how to coax information out of even the most recalcitrant prisoner. Rick would often dismiss his interpreter and sit with a prisoner, all night if necessary, sharing cigarettes and relentlessly breaking down the man's resistance with quiet conversation and canny negotiation. The best kind of information was the kind given willingly, and Rick specialized in the kind of psychological cajolery that invariably produced it. As the rest of the team went to bed, Rick sat down to pull what in college we used to call an "all-nighter" with his VC lieutenant.

My problem was guilt. I couldn't bring myself to retire to a soft bunk while Rick stayed up with the prisoner, so I foolishly decided to sit it out with him. I figured I would be able to offer Rick a sort of unspoken moral support and the knowledge that his work was not going unnoticed. I wasn't going to be one of those officers who fucked off while his men did the dirty jobs, no sir. So I pulled a chair up to my desk in the interrogation office and leaned back to watch over Rick while he talked to the prisoner under a single desk light across the room. It was a mistake to lean back of course, because I fell asleep instantly. It had been one of the most grueling (and most fulfilling, I might add) days of my life, what with predawn raids on An Tan whorehouses, snipers, shooting at children, and unscheduled trips to retrieve sexually active interpreters in Quang Ngai City.

The next thing I knew Rick was shaking my shoulder. "Look, sir, I appreciate your being here, but you're snoring so loud you're disturbing us. Go to bed, sir, and I'll have my interrogation report on your desk in the morning, okay?"

I was too exhausted to argue. So much for my show of support for Rick. I shuffled back to my bunk and fell asleep again before I could remove my boots.

# CHAPTER 21

# Teammates

I was looking forward to the time when I could bring my men back to visit the IPW section at Chu Lai for a stand-down party. It would be my first real chance to show off my status as a brigade team chief and act superior to the poor staff officers, like snotty Lieutenant Buttroon, who had to stay behind inside the division base camp. Was this petty and immature of me? It sure was. But I remembered how envious I used to be of brigade MIT commanders when they came strutting back to Chu Lai all full of themselves, and I wanted the pleasure of being the obnoxious, arrogant object of someone else's envy for once.

The opportunity finally arose about six weeks after I had been at LZ Bayonet. My men and I were due to be paid, and since we were supposed to collect our money back at division anyway, Captain Steele decided to use the occasion to put on a barbecue dinner for the team at the same time. In the letter I wrote to my wife after we returned late that night, here is how I described the first part of our memorable visit:

We all got into a 3/4-ton truck I had borrowed for the trip (which must be the oldest, grungiest one in the Americal) and set off for Chu Lai. Everyone was in a good mood, so the men felt justified in reaching out to pinch the bottoms of all the young girls riding bicycles on Highway 1, making catcalls at passing MPs, giving the finger to every officer they saw on the road and throwing old beer cans out the back of the truck at the guards on the main gate. When we pulled into [MID headquarters], they piled out, clomped into the orderly room, bullied everyone ahead of them out of the line, loudly demanded their pay and insulted the pay officer (our old friend Lt. Buttroon) for his slowness.

Then, because the men wanted to go on a buying spree, we scrambled back in the truck and hit all of the three PX's in Chu Lai like a thunderstorm - accumulating nearly an entire truckload of beer, liquor, soda, candy, dirty magazines and potato chips (in addition to the 100 pounds of equipment they stole from the MID supply room while I was in getting paid). One of my men even managed to get drunk before he even left the first PX (by sitting down behind the beer bins, opening cans with his bayonet and downing several cans in less than five minutes). We only knew where he was because he slugged the MP who caught him stealing the beer. I had to convince the MP to give him a break because he was leaving for the States the next day, which was a lie of course. As I told you in another letter, the men in my team are great interrogators, but when they get time off—or get paid—they are pure-bred hell-raisers.

And so they were. They proved it once again at the stand-down party that evening. After the barbecue, during which two of my interrogators got into a food fight and Sergeant Bo threw up in the lap of Major Lee, the MID commander, everyone sat down in the newly constructed IPW recreation hootch to watch a movie. I don't remember the title or the stars, but I do remember Timmy Lawson, one of my most emotionally unstable men, jumping in front of the screen and pulling his pants down to moon the assembled group as the opening credits rolled. He was the hit of the show with everyone except, of course, the tight-lipped Major Lee and Captain Steele. "Can't you control them better?" Steele whispered to me during the movie.

I shrugged elaborately. "Was anybody ever able to control these guys?"

When Wayne Bingham, loaded to his tonsils with beer, picked that evening to tell Major Lee "exactly what's wrong with this whole goddam, shit-ass MI detachment," however, I decided it was time for MIT #3 to make a graceful exit. My men's reputation for being a pack of rabid party animals was clearly intact.

I made apologies and thank-you's all around and gathered them up to load onto the back of the truck. I decided to take the wheel because I was the only one left sober. As we pulled out of the Chu Lai main gate and turned left onto Highway 1, it belatedly occurred to me that we might easily encounter sniper fire along the dark, empty stretch of road running down to the LZ Bayonet. My men were obviously in no condition to win, or even conduct, a firefight. As soon as the thought hit me, I heard a few rifle reports out to the west of the highway and saw little winks of muzzle flashes. Just as I feared, we were getting pot-shotted by the local VC marksmen, out for an easy kill, I pressed the accelerator pedal to the floor, but the truck merely lumbered on with no increase in speed. "I think there's some kind of fucking governor on this fucking machine," Jack Casey shouted in the cab next to me, "you can't fucking go any faster." Even under the influence of his prodigious drinking that night, Jack was still trying to play big brother to me.

In the back of the truck, the men of MIT #3 leaped into action—or, rather, they tripped, flailed, and blundered into action, yelling in drunken panic to each other and fumbling chaotically for their M-16s stacked under one of the bench seats. "Return fire! Return fire!" I heard Rick Schwartz screech as he discharged an entire magazine into the darkness—on the wrong side of the truck, of course. Then they all started firing their weapons at full automatic in all directions, including ahead of the truck and into the sky. I really broke into a sweat, though, when they accidentally pumped a couple of rounds through the floorboards of the truck bed. If I didn't get us out of there, they were going to disable the vehicle by riddling the axle. I stomped and kicked at the accelerator in frustration, and suddenly the truck lurched forward. I had apparently broken the governor, and now we could leave those snipers (who at this point posed less of a threat than my trigger-happy men) in the dust. I believe I pushed that ancient three-quarter-ton up to sixty mph that night, an Indianapolis Raceway qualifying speed under the circumstances, but I was too busy keeping my swaying, rattling truck on the road to check the speedometer carefully.

The next morning, I was painfully awakened by someone's portable radio playing the pounding strains of "We Gotta Get Out of This Place" by The Animals. If any song could be said to be the anthem of the homesick Vietnam soldier, this was it. AFVN Radio, the U.S. government-run station originating in Saigon, aired all the latest rock hits along with news broadcasts and military messages, but it was the bizarre military messages that remain most clearly in my memory today. It would have been funny if it weren't so pathetic—commercials, like the ones for flashy cars and laundry products we heard on our radios back home, were of course irrelevant in a combat zone. The government didn't need the advertising revenue, and its captive listeners couldn't buy anything anyway. But old habits die hard, and some dim bulb in the AFVN hierarchy probably decided that, since Americans were already accustomed to hearing advertising over their airwaves, why not insert tidbits of military advice where commercials would normally be found? "Great idea!" some general probably said, and the result was an absolutely hilarious yet eerily familiar mix of radio songs, news and messages like these:

(Cheery jingle music playing in the background) "You've got a friend in your insect repellant/Use it in the daytime, and i-i-in the night/Your friend is your insect repellant/It'll keep your dengue fever out of sight!"

(Loud drumbeat) "Remember, Monday (echo: Monday, Monday) is malaria pill day! One big yellow tablet, you GIs, keeps you healthy for a week! Don't fall ill like the gooks—use your pill! This message brought to you by the MACV medical command."

(Sung to the tune of a popular Chevrolet commercial) "Reenlist in the USA/Six more months/and you get bonus pay!"

(Music) "When you're feelin' low/and you're feelin'

blue/Don't let muddy water/get into you. (Voiceover) Remember you poor grunts humpin' out in the boonies, don't forget to use your iodine capsules to purify the water you get in the field. Even if you're too tired, no extra effort at all is required to just open your fatigue pocket, take out the capsule and drop it into that muddy water."

Madison Avenue's finest it wasn't. In fact, these trite jingles and lead-footed exhortations were downright embarrassing to listen to, even if we had no choice. Still, I wrote them down at the time, and they have stuck in my brain ever since, and that's what effective advertising is supposed to do. Even today, I think of malaria pills on Monday mornings.

On that morning over twenty years ago, however, I had other things on my mind. I had not yet solved the problem, for instance, of getting stubborn prisoners to talk. I made it clear to the men from the beginning that I wouldn't tolerate torture of any kind. No beatings, no fingernail removals, no hooking anyone up to a field telephone and cranking the handle to produce electric shocks. Enough of that went on out in the field, where frustrated grunts frequently vented their anger on helpless detainees. Here at the brigade level, I was encountering many more injured prisoners than I had seen at division. We were closer to the field now, and closer to the contorted face of brutality lurking under the surface of men under stress. In my experience, though, torture was counterproductive as well as being against the Geneva Convention rules. Prisoners who were being mistreated would, if they were smart, simply make up information to satisfy their captors. It's what I would have done under the same circumstances. We had a hard enough time verifying detainees' often vague and uninformed stories without having to worry about deliberate fabrications. Generally speaking, a prisoner who spoke voluntarily gave more accurate and coherent information, and I tried to keep this in mind whenever I got pissed off at particular prisoner who resisted interrogation.

We had one like that in the cage now. He was a junior noncommissioned officer from a VC main force unit that had been providing material and troop support to the local-yokel VC forces operating near LZ Bayonet. We suspected that this man (let's call him Nguyen) knew the details of a unique "rental" arrangement between main and local force units, whereby the main force unit would lend mortars and gun crews to the local guys in exchange for local labor crews to build underground bunker complexes out in the jungle. This way the local VC would be able to mount effective mortar attacks on us with the help of their more sophisticated main force comrades, and the main force troops could avoid getting their hands dirty with manual labor.

It was a good deal all around (except for us, of course, because we were the targets), and we wanted to know more about how it worked. This skinny noncom Nguyen, however, had been tight-lipped about it ever since he had been brought in two days before. He wouldn't budge, no matter how long we talked to him, and soon we would be required to ship him up to division. It was time, I thought, to reach into my bag of tricks and try to emulate my old interrogation mentor from division IPW, Tom Guggenschaffer.

Accordingly, I began to set my plan in motion. I removed the magazine from my .45, shoved it into my holster and strode resolutely down to the cage. I told one of the day duty interrogators what I had in mind, and he then went into the cage to find Nguyen. After the interrogator had been inside one of the little interview hootches talking to him for about twenty minutes, I put on my most ferocious Tom Guggenschaffer face and started shouting at the top of my voice. "Where is that fucking gook motherfucker? I'm gonna kill that son of a bitch!" Brandishing the unloaded automatic, I bulled my way into the cage in a feigned frenzy, pushing frightened detainees out of the way and calling out Nguyen's name. Then I switched to Vietnamese curses and shouts (the few I knew, anyway) and kicked open the door of the interrogation hootch. By prearrangement, my interrogator tried to act as a peacemaker, pleading with me to spare poor Nguyen. In its own crude way, this was a variation on the Mutt-and-Jeff routine that those two MI background investigators had pulled on me when I was still at Georgetown ROTC.

Pretending to ignore the interrogator, I hauled Nguyen out of his chair and pitched him across the tiny room. I pulled back the cocking slide of the .45, which made a satisfyingly menacing sound, and jammed the muzzle into his mouth while holding him up against the wall with my free hand. "Talk you shit-ass or I'll splatter your brains!" I screamed into his terrified face. Tom Guggenschaffer would have heartily approved of my impersonation of him. It seemed to work, too. Nguyen burst into tears and dropped to his knees. He hugged my legs, crying and praying for mercy. He called on his ancestors to help him. He thrashed around on the floor in fear. He babbled and cried and blubbered.

He did everything, in fact, but talk.

After Nguyen composed himself, he went back to his chair. I let the interrogator "convince" me to leave, and waited in the office for word that Nguyen had finally agreed to reveal details of the mortar rental deal. No one could have been that terrorized, I thought, and continue to be silent. But I was wrong. In about ten minutes the interrogator emerged to tell me that Nguyen inexplicably still refused to talk. Threats to bring back the "crazy lieutenant" only produced more crying and begging on Nguyen's part, but no offer of information. It looked like I had failed, and I couldn't help thinking that I would never be the passionate natural actor Tom Guggenschaffer had been. My heart, I guess, just hadn't been in it. There was nothing else I could do, so I instructed the interrogator to transfer the incredibly stubborn Nguyen up to division. Word of my ineffective attempt at intimidation spread quickly, and later I found out that my act became known around the team as "Lieutenant Smith's trick that never works," even though I was too embarrassed ever to try it again. It was clear I had no career on Broadway in my future.

# CHAPTER 22

# Losing It

One cool, sunny morning toward the end of March, I woke up with the delicious feeling of not having much to do. Things had been quiet the night before ("too quiet" as the soldiers in the movies used to say just before all hell broke loose), with only a few detainees filtering into the cage and no significant action or contacts reported by any of our battalions operating in the field. All seemed to be well with the interpreters, the interrogators, Major Kanka at the brigade TOC, and even Captain Steele back at Chu Lai base. My world was serene for once.

Around LZ Bayonet, the morning routine was beginning. Vietnamese day workers were trooping through the front gate and helicopters were warming up on their various pads. A forward air controller's light plane floated overhead like a seagull, drifting almost silently to the west where the day's targets lay. I poured myself a cup of coffee and strolled down the hallway of my hootch to the bunker attached to the end of the building. I passed many pleasant evenings out there chatting with Jack Casey and some of the CI agents in what we called the "Bunker Club." I rested my cup on the sandbag revetment and looked out past wooden beams bracing the wall to the view of Chu Lai airfield I could see through the bunker's firing ports. From a distance of several miles, it looked uncharacteristically peaceful over there.

I will describe what happened next in the words I wrote in a letter to my wife later that day. After all these years, my language seems a bit overheated to me, but since I wrote the letter with the incident fresh in my mind, these words still seem to describe best what I saw:

Dimly at first, but with increasing urgency, the sound of a long, sputtering scream [came through] the still air—a shrill, high-pitched noise like a giant whistle—and then several more shrieks, and I looked up to see black, needle-like silhouettes of 122mm VC rockets pass overhead and plummet directly into the jet hangars three miles away. Several tremendous flashes appeared, and seconds later the metallic thumps came, shaking everything with many rippling shock waves that could be seen radiating from the points of impact.

Great voluminous billows of black smoke from exploded jet fuel and burning gas belched from the distant hangars, and as the base sirens went off in a wail, ammunition in the fire began to [detonate] into the confusion, casting sparklers, tracers and flashes out hundreds of feet from the rocketed area. A few more secondary explosions came, and just as suddenly as it started, the fire subsided, leaving only smouldering metal and wood to disturb the returned peace of the early-morning camp.

While I was gazing at this ghastly yet fascinating sight, the first rocket barrage I had witnessed from such a protected vantage point, Jack Casey trotted down the hallway to stand next to me. "Kinda beautiful, isn't it," he said in a low voice, "even though somebody over there's getting the holy shit kicked out of them. Sure makes me glad I'm here instead of Chu Lai." I mumbled some reply and wondered a little sadly to myself if Jack and I hadn't been in the combat zone too long. Although I sympathized in a vague sort of way with the men who might have been killed or wounded by those rockets—after all, I had been a Chu Lai target myself not so long ago—I felt no strong bond with my fellow soldiers. Rockets in the morning were their problem, not mine. If somebody over there hadn't awakened quickly enough and made it to a bunker, well, hell, those were the breaks of the combat game we were all playing. I was snug in the Bunker Club with a steaming mug of coffee in my hand, and my ass hadn't been killed.

That was all I cared about, and it worried me that that was all I cared about. I didn't remember feeling that way when I first arrived in country, but it looked like nine months of random death and miscellaneous destruction had scrambled my emotional connections.

I experienced more evidence of growing internal conflict later that day, after the evening log birds dumped another load of detainees on us. I had grabbed a quick dinner at the brigade mess hall and was on my way into the cage to see how our interrogations were proceeding. Three steps inside the compound, I stopped short—something was wrong. What happened to MP guards? Why was the office empty? Where the hell was everybody? Instead of the constant noise and movement of a normal night's prisoner screening, there was only silence and semidarkness around the cage. I drew my .45 and snapped the cocking slide. For all I knew, the prisoners might have overpowered the guards and escaped, or worse, they might be holding my men hostage. Without thinking (a much smarter move at this juncture would have been to go for some help) I moved deeper into the compound with my pistol ready.

As I tiptoed forward through the dimness, I remembered Tom Guggenschaffer telling me once that the MPs had turned down the lights and withdrawn from a cage he was working in when they thought some kind of atrocity was about to take place. Because many MPs were former combat infantrymen, filling out the tail end of their tours with POW guard duty, they had no love for either Victor Charlie or the niceties of the Geneva Convention. Tom said that rather than stop IPW interrogators from torturing or abusing detainees, some MPs simply pulled out and went for a walk. That way they couldn't be called later as witnesses, either. Could the MPs have done that here? If so, where were my interrogators and what were they doing now?

Up ahead, near the line of interrogation hootches, I heard a mixture of sounds I couldn't identify at once. Chopping? Groaning? Moving closer, I caught a glimpse of one of my men, Timmy Lawson, behind the last hootch. The top of his head was level with the ground, and another head, a Vietnamese one, was visible near him. As I turned the corner, I saw Lawson standing in a deep shell crater, pistol-whipping a prisoner whose hands were tied. Lawson's legs were straddled wide apart as he swung his arm left and right in a looping arc. In his hand was a .45 automatic, and fixed at the barrel end of the flailing pistol was a sharp sight blade that slashed the prisoner's face with every powerful swipe. One of the prisoner's jowls had come unhinged at the cheek, and it flapped around in bloody rhythm with Lawson's hysterical blows.

Lawson was screaming questions almost incoherently at the tottering man, but I could see no interpreter present, and it was clear that my interrogator had lost any semblance of control. From the beginning of my time with the team, I had noticed that Lawson seemed more volatile and moody, more "peculiar" than the others in a way I couldn't identify easily.

Holstering my pistol, I jumped into the crater. I intended to disarm Lawson and pull him down from behind, but when I wrapped my arms around his thick torso, grappling for the pistol, my motion turned somehow into an awkward hug. I had also intended to order Lawson to stop, but the harsh words that were supposed to come out of my mouth were transformed into sobs. I stood there, holding Lawson in my arms and crying for what had happened to him. To me. To the prisoner. We had all been at war for too long. Lawson dropped his red-tipped pistol and slumped in my grasp. Then he cried, too.

A few minutes later, I sent Lawson back to the barracks area and tried to give the prisoner first aid. Naturally I couldn't remember a single word of any of the medical instruction I had received at Fort Benning and ROTC summer camp (had there been a class on fixing cheek flaps?), so I handed the man my handkerchief to press against his dangling jowl and walked him over to the brigade aid station to be treated. I said nothing to him, but we both knew that he could report his mistreatment at Lawson's hands to higher authorities, and the severity of his wound would back up his story. But perhaps because I had rescued him, or because he had expected even worse treatment after being captured (detainees routinely asked us when we were going to eat them), the prisoner never spoke up after I had him transferred up to division IPW the next day. At least I never heard of the incident again.

Similarly, I didn't speak to Lawson about that nightmare in the shell crater. I didn't think I needed to remind him that what he did to a helpless prisoner was unforgivably cruel as well as a blatant violation of the laws of war. I had no plans to report his illegal actions to anyone, either, and to this day I'm not certain why. Maybe I took my role as the mother-hen protector of the men too seriously. Maybe I understood too well how close to the edge we all were. Months of handling sheeplike prisoners who were completely in our power brought out the hidden sadist in all of us, as it would have in anyone. I could only keep an eye on Lawson to make sure he didn't crack like that again. He would perform no more solitary interrogations while I was there.

What I did do that night, however, was walk back to the cage to have a talk with the MP captain in charge of the guards. As I expected, everything was proceeding normally at the cage, as if nothing had happened, when I returned from the aid station. My interpreters and interrogators were working their way through the day's detainees, and the MPs were back at their duty stations. I still had no idea where everyone had been hiding while Lawson was brutalizing his prisoner, and I decided not to waste any time trying to find out. To the MP captain, who may have believed Lawson was conducting the kind of interrogation of which I approved, I said, "The next time you think something like that is going to happen, call me. If you can't find me, keep your men on duty until you do. I don't ever want to walk in and find an empty cage again, okay?"

"Okay, if that's the way you want it" was his only reply.

A few minutes later I repeated those instructions to the rest of the team. There were no arguments. Up to that point I could only guess what went on in the minds of soldiers who mistreated prisoners. I had heard that troops in the field were prone to engage in casual brutality, but their behavior was at least understandable because they had lost buddies to the VC and NVA prisoners they took. But after that it was a different story—at brigade and division IPW sections we were intelligence professionals. We weren't supposed to let emotions interfere with our duty to extract information without cruelty. I knew that, along with the enlisted men of MIT #3, I had been exiled to the lowest possible rung of the MI ladder—you couldn't wear MI insignia and be assigned to any unit below the level of brigade—but that didn't change anything. As professionals, we were expected to behave accordingly, no matter what everyone else around us was doing.

That's what I believed, anyway, until the day I lost control myself. After that, I finally understood, if I could not completely accept, how it could happen. Not more than a week after the Lawson incident, a young prisoner entered the LZ Bayonet cage who would try the patience and good intentions of a bishop. He was about sixteen years old, a bony, smartass village boy from An Tan who had been recruited by the local VC to scout LZ Bayonet. We knew that because an alert MP had spotted him slinking around the mess hall, drawing a crude map of our base camp on his palm with a ballpoint pen. He must have come in through the front gate with the regular morning crowds of Vietnamese day workers, few of whom were ever searched or even checked for IDs. The MP turned the kid in, and from his first moment in custody, he pissed everybody off with his defiant attitude. He refused to explain the map sketched on his hand. He wouldn't reveal his name. He wouldn't tell us where he lived, although it was certain he was from An Tan. Most enraging of all, however, he kept a wide, fixed grin on his face while being questioned. As I sat in on his interrogation, fuming at his intransigence, I couldn't help thinking of all the snotty teenagers I had met since I stopped being one myself. I could see why my parents and teachers had gotten so furious at me if I acted anything like this annoying little prick.

American soldiers in Vietnam were also constantly being exposed to gangs of "Saigon cowboys," the generic term for South Vietnamese males in their late teens who went joyriding around the countryside on motorbikes and motorcycles with their giggling girlfriends on the back. These punks were clearly of draft age, and yet they somehow retained their civilian status (and pleasures) while eighteen- and nineteen-year-old Americans were getting their arms and legs blown off defending their country. This leering kid, although he worked for the VC, became mixed up in my mind with all the Saigon cowboys I had ever seen and hated (and envied), all the flip, smart-aleck teenagers I had known, and even all the draft dodgers back in the World, who I imagined were blowing dope, fucking their girlfriends, and comfortably watching the war on TV while I ducked rockets and shaved out of a helmet in a shithole twelve thousand miles from home.

Does this sound like I was flipping out at last? Yes, it does to me. Did I let this kid, who was, after all, only a symbol in my mind, get under my skin so much that I lost objectivity and professionalism? Yes again. At that moment I felt nearly a year's worth of frustration, rage, fear, wrath, and disgust overwhelming my emotional defenses. I wanted to kill the snippy little bastard with my bare hands. "Let me take him!" I told my interrogator. I pulled the kid out of his chair and frog-marched him over to a nearby bunker. I closed the door and untied his hands. We were alone. He stood there on the dirt floor and rubbed his wrists, looking quizzically at me but still grinning infuriatingly. Almost gently, I took his hand and turned it palm-up. "This is a map," I said in English, "and you're going to tell me who ordered you to draw it, aren't you?" The kid backed away, his grin beginning to quiver at the corners. He spoke little English, but he recognized my menacing tone.

"Aren't you?" I shouted, and clouted him across the side of his head with my fist. "C'mon, punk, talk to me!" I popped a short punch into his breadbasket, propelling him back across the bunker. But he was still grinning. A red tide flooded my eyes, and I threw a vicious left hook to his jaw. Then I stepped up, braced him against the sandbag wall, and methodically began to slap his face hard with both hands. First left, then right, then left, then right again. Over and over like a metronome. With each rotation of my shoulders, each trajectory of my arms, each fleshy impact of my open hands on his face, I felt an almost ecstatic release of pressure. This must have been what that asshole Lawson felt when he was pistol-whipping his prisoner, I thought dimly, but the unfortunate comparison only added force to my blows.

The kid, his smirk long erased, tried to cover up his face with his arms, but each time, I roughly yanked them down to his sides. "You're just gonna stand there and take it, you little fucker," I said, smiling now myself. With each blow, his face was getting puffier, and his eyes were beginning to glaze over—and then I felt a hand grip my forearm and heard Rick Schwartz say, "Stop it, Lieutenant Smith. That's enough, okay?" Rick was doing for me what I had done for Tim Lawson. He led me out of the bunker and sat me down outside. My breath came in short bursts, and I was sweating freely. Rick took the prisoner back to the cage and left me alone. No more was ever said about the incident, but I knew Rick had saved me from beating the kid senseless and possibly harming him permanently.

Later I realized that I had actually been enjoying myself in that bunker. Hitting the kid had been a pure, sadistic pleasure, and I could see how even the most civilized person could get into the habit of mistreatment. It also scared the shit out of me that I enjoyed myself. I didn't like the person I was becoming. I promised myself I would never lose control like that again, and I didn't.

One day shortly after that, I got a note from John Ackerman, a hometown friend of mine who was a platoon leader with the 198th Brigade. The note said he and his men were staying in a "stand-down hotel" outside Chu Lai for a few days, and could I come out to visit him? John and I had gone to grade school, high school, and college together, and even served in the same ROTC unit. Now, by chance, we found ourselves in the same brigade of the same division in far-off Vietnam (we had learned about this from letters our respective parents back in Garden City wrote to us earlier). It would be great to see a familiar face, so I sent a note back, saying I would drive out the next evening. The Americal Division maintained stand-down hotels as in-country R & R centers for troops who had been in the field for long periods of time. They were often built in isolated locations outside the main base camps, however, because the army seemed to be nervous about the soldiers' unruly behavior while they were off duty.

I could understand the army's fear as soon as I drove my jeep into the hotel compound west of Chu Lai the following evening. Several long, two-story barracks hastily constructed of raw wood were set into a jungle clearing. Music was blaring from every window, accompanied by loud singing and peals of drunken laughter. I saw the shadows of women as well as men moving among the trees. The sound of beer bottles breaking could be heard every few seconds, like a college fraternity party back in the World. I was told later that second-rate Filipino rock bands were dispatched out there regularly to perform, and that droves of Vietnamese prostitutes considered the place to be a second home. I met John in the dirt parking lot, and we sat down on a log to catch up on old (and new) times. During our conversation, he mentioned that he had never received any information back about prisoners his platoon had turned in during field operations. "You know, we pick these dinks up, and I tell my guys to lay off them so they'll cooperate with the intelligence people, but then the dinks go to prison camps, and we don't hear a goddamn word about what they had to say," he told me. Unfortunately, John was right. The IPW system was designed to extract information, but not to disseminate it back to the capturing units. All of my interrogation reports were sent *up* the line—to the brigade S-2 officer, to division, to I Corps, and eventually to Saigon—but no one seemed to care about passing that information back down the line to the companies and platoons that picked up the prisoners in the first place. How could I convince a platoon leader like John to protect his prisoners when he received no direct benefit from doing so?

Right then I resolved to get prisoner information back to my friend. I would keep an eye out for prisoners who came from his company or platoon (you could tell from the capture tags), and make sure I sent a copy of the interrogation report back to him. Why was I at brigade, after all, if not to help out troops in the field? John's men would at least get to see the results of their efforts, and maybe even learn something from the interrogation reports that could save lives. And if the system worked with my friend's unit, I planned to expand it to other small units throughout the brigade. When I left John that night, I told him to expect to hear from me soon.

It was a well-intentioned plan, but a doomed one. A few

days later, when a prisoner captured by John's platoon came into the cage at LZ Bayonet, I belatedly realized that all such interrogation reports were automatically classified confidential or secret and therefore restricted to those who had army security clearances. I couldn't just throw a confidential report like that into the brigade mail distribution bin and have it shipped out to my friend in the jungle somewhere. It would be seen and handled by too many unauthorized people. Still, there ought to be something I could do. I then sat down at my desk and tried to summarize the information we had learned from the prisoner into a sanitized report for my friend, but it simply wouldn't work. Stripped of its classified content, the report was useless and pointless. I gave it up, settling for a brief note to John telling him his prisoner had arrived in good shape but that I wasn't permitted to reveal what we had learned. My friend did not reply, and I don't blame him. We were both victims of an intelligence system that, sometimes, wasn't very intelligent.

At about this time, I also engaged in another failed intelligence venture. At various times since I had been at LZ Bayonet, I noticed Vietnamese children roaming around, selling little bags of marijuana to the troops. Drug abuse in Vietnam was just beginning to reflect the same problem back in the United States, but the army hadn't yet taken official notice of pot in its ranks. It occurred to me that the VC would be smart to distribute marijuana at rock-bottom prices just before they intended to attack a base camp. Many of the bunker-line guards and reaction forces might then be under the influence of the drug, and the VC could enter unscathed. It made sense to me, and the VC, who were never shy about exploiting American frailties, might have thought of it already. If the price of pot being peddled in base camps could then be charted and matched with the frequency of VC attacks, there might be a direct relationship—the lower the price, the higher the likelihood of attack. I wrote down my suggestions for a trial effort to chart marijuana prices in a personal report to Captain Steele, but it came back twenty-four hours later with a note of refusal. I called Steele to find out why, and he said, "It's the most ridiculous idea I ever heard of, and besides, the army would never admit that American soldiers are smoking pot. So forget it." Well, maybe my idea was a bit farfetched, but no more so than the army's belief that its soldiers in Vietnam weren't getting stoned.

I had by then been at LZ Bayonet long enough to feel comfortable in my job, however, so I didn't let such small setbacks bother me. I was actually beginning to like it in Vietnam. I assumed I would be in command of MIT #3 for several more months, and I thought I had plenty of time left to improve my professional skills.

As usual, I was wrong.

# CHAPTER 23

# Getting Out

It was April 1969, the beginning of springtime in Vietnam and back in the World. My wife, who had been working in Knoxville as a junior-high-school teacher since I'd left (and saving every tax-free nickel of the salary allotment I sent home), wrote me that she had rented a little white Cape Cod near her school. She mailed me a snapshot, and seeing the house with its diminutive lawn and two large trees plunged me into a wave of homesickness. I had been gone for more than ten months, and I could tell from magazines and newspapers that, in that critical time, the entire country had been transformed—open drug use, hippies, peace marches, and civil disobedience on an unprecedented scale, free love, fem lib, black power, radical environmentalism, and a new level of social awareness I had never experienced. The world had turned many times over while I was in exile twelve thousand miles away. I wanted to go home.

And then I found out that I would be going home—soon. Rather than passively pine away for her absent husband, my enterprising wife had found an army education program that allowed soldiers who were accepted into accredited colleges or graduate schools to be granted an early release from service. My wife's successful effort to have me enrolled in a graduate political-science program, combined with my prolonged training regimen before I went overseas and my two-year active duty enlistment period, fortunately dovetailed to permit me to leave Vietnam more than a month and a half before my scheduled rotation date. Suddenly I was "short," army parlance for someone with a quickly diminishing number of days left in country.

Being short does funny things to you. It makes you cautious and fearful in situations where you normally wouldn't be. The hope—now made real by a definite departure date—that you might actually survive your time in a combat zone turns you into an instant sniveling coward. The army recognized this, and in Vietnam the common practice was to withdraw men from dangerous duty as they got closer to their DEROS (date of estimated return from overseas). The army and the man's comrades don't want jumpy, hesitant soldiers around where they can do any harm. My problem was that, contrary to normal practice, I found myself more exposed to harm at the end of my tour than at the beginning. As I approached DEROS, I should have been back at division, sipping cool drinks in the officers club and shuffling papers instead of leading a brigade intelligence team in the MI equivalent of "the field." All I could do was pray a little and try not to show how terrified I was that I could be wounded or blown away before I climbed on the freedom bird for home.

Word spread quickly that I was getting out. Captain Steele called to say that my replacement would be sent over in several days, and that I should take an inventory of the equipment under my control to sign it over. A thick set of orders arrived through the mail distribution, assigning me to Fort Lewis, Washington, for the purpose of being released from active duty. Captain Cartera, one of my least favorite S-2 officers at the brigade TOC, took to making snide cracks about my courage, now that I was getting short. "Watch out for those rockets, Smitty [a nickname I hated]," he said, "they're gonna make you shit in your pants now." The hardest part, however, was telling the men of MIT #3 that I would be leaving. I had made it a point to keep them out of harm's way as much as possible, despite pressures from above, and now I had to turn their safety and welfare over to some unknown lieutenant. Their reaction at first was typical of the men I had come to know—cynical, detached and low-key. They congratulated me on my good luck and speculated on how much sex and booze I would be enjoying while they were stuck in a toilet like LZ Bayonet.

That night, though, I heard them getting roaring drunk over in their barracks across from my hootch. Somewhere they had "liberated" an entire three-quarter-ton trailer full of beer in rusted cans, and had gladly spent nearly all of their spare time in previous weeks rubbing the rust off with Brillo pads. Now the beer was flowing, and shortly before midnight a delegation—Rick Schwartz, Timmy Lawson, and Wayne Bingham—stumbled over to my room to talk. "We would like to ask you to re-up, Lieutenant Smith," Rick said with as much besotted dignity as he could muster, "so you can come back to MIT #3, okay?"

I knew what he was referring to. If I agreed to extend my combat zone tour by six months, the army would guarantee that I could keep the same leadership position after I returned to Vietnam from a thirty-day leave at home. It was the army's way of encouraging people to stay in jobs they had learned well, and Rick was asking on behalf of the men if, after a furlough, I would stay on at MIT #3 rather than rotating home permanently. I was immensely flattered and moved that they didn't want to lose me, and I said so. But I also told the three men that I had only been married six months before I came to Vietnam, and that I missed my wife and family, and home terribly. "I have to go, guys," I said.

"We know that, sir, but we just wanted to give it a try," Rick said, and led the others back to the barracks. I have been nursing a guilt complex about that night ever since.

One day, as I was trying to count for my successor the rifles, gas masks, water cans, tarpaulins, ammo boxes, jeeps, desks, cots, pencils, stencils, report forms, sandbag stores, spare helmets, ponchos, C-ration cases, and toilet paper rolls in the possession of MIT #3, I received a surprise visit from the Indian, my half-Cherokee friend from combat center days and the only officer of the original five besides myself who was left in Vietnam—Warren Witzener was back home in a veteran's hospital somewhere, learning to use a prosthetic arm; Mike Pojeski had gone nuts and was stripped of his commission; Phil Talbott was doing hard time in Fort Leavenworth. The Indian, who had heard only recently that I was at the 198th Brigade, told me he had been out in the field for the last ten months, either at the head of his infantry platoon or doing special reconnaissance work he wouldn't specify. He was even more taciturn than I remembered, but he did let on that he didn't think he would survive his tour, which like mine originally, was to run another month and a half. I said good-bye to him, thinking that I would be the only one of the five members of the ill-fated combat center "club" to make it home undisgraced and in one piece. I was wrong, but it took me twenty years to find that out. Last year, I finally summoned the courage to look up the Indian's name in the Vietnam War Memorial files in Washington, D.C. His name wasn't on that dark, polished stone wall, and I'm sure the helpful records clerk at the memorial was quite accustomed to seeing middle-aged men like me burst into tears when they got good news like that.

Now, at the end of my tour, was the time for nostalgic looks back, and the Indian's visit reminded me that I hadn't seen the old combat center since I left it nearly a year before. So, with the spare time I was beginning to have, I drove over to Chu Lai to revisit some places that gave me my first impressions of the Americal. In a letter to my parents, I described my feelings and impressions:

Now it's almost over, and now I can come back to life. In some ways it seems like a century ago that I arrived, dirty and tired, at the dinky little Chu Lai airstrip. . . . Chu Lai was little more than a construction area then, with the Marines still here in large numbers and the scattered brigades operating as independent units. Now the Marines are gone, all the brigades are consolidated from the old Task Force Oregon, we have a big air terminal (even R&R flights leave directly from Chu Lai now), we have a bank, an American Express office and the base looks like a big rear-area rest home. The crummy, sandswept little combat center I sweated through with my friends has been transformed into a new, modern, (paved, even!) classroom complex (and the classrooms are AIR-CONDITIONED!) with snack bars, chapels, tailor shops and 'combat' and 'non-combat' courses to choose from. So many new faces, changes.

I added a few details in a letter to my wife at about the same time:

> When I was roaming around the combat center, I bumped into a fresh new 2nd lieutenant, just arriving in country. He talked to me like I was some kind of old World War I veteran, asked me all the stupid questions I asked people when I first got here, and almost fainted when I told him that our final 'practical exercise' at the end of the combat center was a real patrol down the beach, outside the Americal perimeter (I even remember we actually took a couple of rounds from some dink out there). He couldn't imagine a time when the center was as primitive as I said it was.

I also drove down to LZ Gator ("poor" LZ Gator, the fire support base that seemed to get so much more than its fair share of enemy poundings) to deliver some good news to a friend of mine from Fort Benning days. I had heard that the division IPW section was looking for an experienced infantry lieutenant with some S-2 time under his belt to work in the office up at Chu Lai. My friend, whom I had visited once or twice while I was at LZ Bayonet, was perfectly suited for this job and could certainly benefit from being taken out of isolated, rocket-torn LZ Gator. When I told Captain Steele I had just the man for him, he quickly arranged for my friend's transfer to IPW and assigned me the pleasant task of informing him in person. My friend, who had a wife and child at home and whose tour still had some months to go, was touchingly grateful for this little bit of string-pulling on my part. He would be (relatively) safe now while he got short.

In Vietnam, a man's replacement was generically nicknamed a "turtle" because he always seemed so slow to arrive. My turtle, baby-faced 2d Lt. John Toby, arrived at LZ Bayonet two weeks before my departure, however, which was plenty of time for me to coinspect and sign over the twenty thousand dollars worth of army property the team owned, and to orient him to his new duties. Toby appeared to be a decent, intelligent young fellow, but like all veteran commanders, I secretly felt he could never measure up to my standard. Would he buck the system to make sure the men were protected from harm? Would he remember to make them check their gas masks? Would he cancel the obligatory evening volleyball game? How could this well-meaning but green butter bar run a unit that I had needed all of my experience to handle? Would the men constantly compare him unfavorably to me? I wouldn't be there to find out the answers.

But if I deluded myself into thinking I was indispensable, I was in for a rude wakeup call. Late one night, about a week before I went home, I awoke to the familiar sounds of my men's boots clumping down the narrow hootch hall. During the time I served at LZ Bayonet, I had been summoned out of bed innumerable times at all hours to tackle a wide variety of tasks. I was used to it. Sometimes one of the men wanted to talk about something personal, but more often it was a unit problem—a special document that needed to be looked at, a crucial bit of information from a late interrogation that I had to run down to the TOC, an early briefing, or any one of a number of expected crises and emergencies that arise in a combat zone.

Grumbling, I pushed the mosquito netting aside, pulled on my trousers and waited for the late visitors to enter my tiny room. The boots kept walking, however, and out in the hall, I could see two of my men making their way to Lieutenant Toby's quarters two alcoves away. What the hell was this? I heard low, excited voices and realized they were telling Toby about whatever this latest emergency was. A few minutes later, Toby, now in full fatigue uniform, walked out with them. The hall was silent again. It was clear then that I was no longer the Old Man who solved all problems and settled all disputes. I had been replaced. Lieutenant Toby, baby face and all, was now the new boss of MIT #3. He was the one my men would go to for help after midnight. A wave of jealousy sloshed over me, but I knew it was for the best. They had asked me to stay in command, and I had told them I was going home. Lieutenant Smith is (symbolically) dead! Long live Lieutenant Toby! I went back to sleep, wondering, despite myself, what the visit had been about.

Still, my tour of duty wasn't quite over yet, and in the few days left to me in country, I would find out there were a couple of interesting loose ends that needed tying up.

# CHAPTER 24

# Settling Up

Three days before departure, I was enjoying an after-lunch mug of coffee in the brigade mess hall and reflecting on the unusually high quality of the food at LZ Bayonet (this is not a satirical comment—the mess sergeant actually seemed to care about what he served), when Captain Cartera from the S-2 office sidled up to my table with a malicious grin on his face.

"Well, Smitty," he said, using the nickname I disliked as much as its user, "I guess you're so short you don't even care about what I've got here." He oh-so-casually displayed a torn piece of paper in his hand.

I tried to be breezy, "You might as well show whatever it is to Lieutenant Toby, sir. I'm so short, I don't even work here anymore."

"Yeah, sure. I'll give it to your turtle, Smitty. But you'd be interested in this. It's a report we got on a high-ranking prisoner they pulled in down at Ly Tin. They say this dink is an NVA major or something—has a lot of good poop about enemy activities in the area."

"A major, you say?" I couldn't help revealing my curiosity. I had never seen a prisoner of that advanced rank during my whole time in country. Despite myself, I envied Lieutenant Toby for getting to interrogate him. Ly Tin, about twenty miles due south of LZ Bayonet, was the district headquarters for the friendly Ruff-Puffs (Regional Forces/Popular Forces) in our tactical zone. I had never gotten around to visiting there.

"Yeah. And they want someone to fly down to Ly Tin to pick this guy up and bring him back to our cage," he said.

"But I guess you're gonna let Lieutenant Toby do it because you're short and scared of a little chopper ride now, right, Smitty?" Cartera was openly mocking me, the sneering son of a bitch, and his mockery hit home because a twenty-mile chopper hop over enemy territory was precisely what I was scared of, with only seventy-two hours to go before I left for home.

To this day I'm not sure of why I did it. Maybe I was feeling excessively guilty over leaving my men behind in Toby's inexperienced hands. Maybe I didn't like the contempt in Cartera's little piggy eyes. In any case, I grabbed the piece of paper (which was a radio report from Ly Tin) out of his hands and said, "I'll go."

Cartera's eyebrow went up. "Okay, Smitty, rustle up a chopper for yourself. And bring the dink back in time to show him to the brigade commander at tonight's briefing."

I arranged at the TOC for a helicopter to pick me up at the cage pad in ten minutes and ran back to the hootch for helmet and weapon. I was going for my last chopper ride. It was a Cayuse light observation helicopter (nickname Loach), a small four-seat model I'd never traveled in before; it was piloted by a young army warrant officer, wearing a huge white cowboy hat over his headphones.

"Hey, sir!" he called out over the turbo whine of the engine, "I hope you don't mind if I do a little jigging in the air on the way down to Ly Tin. It throws the snipers off."

"No problem. Just get me there and back—and I'm taking a prisoner back with me, okay?"

"Plenty of room, sir. Hold on now."

The "little jigging" he mentioned turned out to be a terrifying, stomach-wrenching series of aerobatics beyond anything I had ever experienced. The cowboy pilot abruptly lifted our Loach to about fifty feet of altitude, tilted the chopper's nose southward, and then began to execute three-dimensional evasive maneuvers designed to baffle anyone on the ground who would try to take a shot at us—a routine hazard of all flights in Vietnam. We dipped. We banked. We rose up and plunged immediately down. We zigged and zagged and rolled and pitched at speeds in excess of one hundred mph. At one point we flew low enough to pass between a pair of tall chimneys on a farmhouse. All I could do was pull my safety harness tighter, grip the engine cowling with my free hand, and hope that potential snipers were getting as dizzy and disoriented from all this as I was.

The pilot bounced our Loach's landing skids onto the packed dirt in front of the Ly Tin district headquarters, and I toppled out, soaked with sweat from helmet liner to bootlaces. "Wait here," I said, "I won't be very long." Inside the long wooden building, tough-looking militiamen lounged around wearing incongruous bits of paramilitary gear over their peasant clothing. Nobody seemed to be in charge. In Vietnamese I identified myself and asked to be shown to the high-ranking NVA prisoner which, according to the report, they had captured three days before. One man led me to a storeroom in the back and pointed to what looked like a heap of bloody clothing on the floor. I leaned over it, and the stench of decayed flesh assaulted my nostrils. The dead man, or what was left of him after several days of rotting in the heat, was clearly beyond interrogation. No one at Ly Tin offered any explanation of what had happened to him, and I decided not to press the issue since I seemed to be the only American around for miles. Had he really been a high-ranking officer? Had he died of wounds inflicted in a firefight before he was captured? Had he died under crude interrogation by these backwoods Ruff-Puffs? I would never know.

But then an idea came to me, the kind of idea that can only come to you after nearly a year in a place like Vietnam. Only much later, when you have settled back into the civilized world, does it occur to you that your thought process at the time was in any way warped. I bent over the body and picked it up in a cross-chest carry. It was light, merely a bag of bones wrapped in frayed cloth and loose flesh. I walked out of the building, and no one stopped me. "Don't take me back to the cage pad," I said to the pilot, "I want you to drop me at the pad next to the colonel's trailer, okay?" Captain Cartera said I should bring the prisoner to the brigade commander's briefing, so that's what I was going to do. I didn't want anyone to accuse me of being so scared of being short that I couldn't complete my last mission.

The pilot stared at me as I strapped myself in with the bloodstained corpse across my lap, but all he said was, "Right, sir."

I don't remember the ride back to LZ Bayonet, but I don't think I'll ever forget the smell and feel of the body harnessed in with me as we whizzed through the air together over Quang Tin Province. When we landed, I picked the corpse up in my arms again and walked toward the brigade commander's trailer where the regular evening briefing was about to begin. I knew who would be inside, and a huge, revengeful grin split my face as I stepped through the doorway. Everybody knew that Cartera had been taunting me lately, and now everybody would get to witness my reply.

I walked past the briefing maps, turned smartly to the left and strode down along the rows of folding chairs to where Captain Cartera was sitting with his head down, examining some report on his clipboard. None of the officers present said a word, although their faces were aghast. It was almost as if they knew something like this was coming.

"Here's your prisoner, sir." I said, and dumped the stinking carcass squarely in Cartera's lap. His reaction was a joy to behold—the clipboard flew into the air, his arms flailed wildly at the body, now sliding to the floor, and he let out a shriek of pure, unmitigated terror. He jumped up and ran out of the trailer, rubbing furiously at his well-starched but now stained trouser legs. I shrugged, smiled at the group, saluted the colonel, and walked out myself. Cartera was already trotting back to his quarters to change his uniform, so I ambled over to the mess hall for some coffee. My part of the briefing, I guessed, was over.

And what the hell, I was short anyway.

The next morning, Captain Steele called and asked me to drive over to see him at Chu Lai. I wondered if he wanted to talk about the Cartera episode, but when I entered Steele's little office an hour later, I could tell something else entirely was on his mind. For one thing, he was smiling at me.

"You're going home tomorrow, Smith, so this will be our last chance to talk. You remember, of course, that just before you were assigned to MIT #3, I gave you an officer efficiency report that wasn't so hot."

"Yes, sir, I remember." How could I forget being called a shitty, disrespectful officer and a disgrace to the army?

"Well, I'm going to do something here that's a little unorthodox. I've written up another OER, one that will supercede—replace, actually—the one you received before. This new one reflects the good work you've done out at the 198th. If you decide at some point that you want to make a career of the army, this OER will allow you to do so."

Steele was obviously uncomfortable telling me all this. Most of the time, he kept his eyes lowered, and he fiddled nervously with a pencil on his desk. But if I had heard him right, he was telling me that I had done so much better at brigade than at division that I had redeemed myself in his eyes. To prove it, he was taking the unprecedented step of tearing up my first, disastrous OER and putting another into the record instead. I had felt for some time that Steele and I were coming to some kind of understanding with each other, possibly even a mild form of mutual respect. I had certainly learned a lot about the problems he faced by being a unit commander myself. And he had seen me grow up a little.

A long time before, back in Georgetown ROTC, one of my military science professors (who was subsequently killed in Vietnam) had told me that I seemed to be the kind of person who was better at leading than following. "When you can't play the rebel, Smith," he said, "when you are in authority yourself, you start to take your responsibilities seriously." Maybe that had finally happened to me at LZ Bayonet. Out there I had been the Old Man, out from under authority's thumb and the arbiter of my own behavior. There was no one to challenge except myself.

"I don't have your new OER finished, Eric," Captain Steele said, using my first name for the first (and now the last) time, "so you'll have to wait until you're back in the States to read it in your file." Months later, I made an appointment at an army records depot in Washington, D.C., where my wife and I were living at the time, and went in to read Captain Steele's comments in my 201 personnel file. I don't remember his exact words after all these years, but I do remember that he told the army I was a better leader than follower, and that I had turned into a pretty damned good officer.

Captain Steele and I had finally made our peace with each other, and not a moment too soon because I was so short I was invisible—I was flying out on the freedom bird the next afternoon.

# CHAPTER 25

# The World

I had said all my good-byes. Now it was time for some hellos.

The C-130 freedom bird to Cam Ranh Bay lifted off the tarmac not far from where an earlier one had dumped me at the end of a runway at the beginning of my tour. I looked down on a sloppy, sprawling, sunlit army base, much larger now than the one I had seen coming in to Chu Lai for the first time. In the years since I returned home, I've kept track of Chu Lai, LZ Bayonet, and that area of I Corps through press accounts and talks with men who went back.

In my piles of clippings and notes, kept carefully folded in a cardboard box with yellowed Vietnam photographs, I have a *Time* magazine article from November 8, 1971, entitled "The America Goes Home."

Last week ... as the wind-driven rain slanted in from the northeast ..., the division commander pulled the lanyard on an artillery piece and officially fired the last round of the Americal in combat. After four years in the field, the Americal is standing down. It is none too soon. Every war produces its hard-luck units, and the Americal, for all the bravery of most of its men, was the G.I. Joe Btfsplk of Vietnam. Soon after the division's headquarters returns to the U.S. this month, the colors will be officially retired and the books closed on this ill-fated outfit. Throughout its existence the division behaved as though plagued by some unknown malignancy. Most notoriously, there ... was Lieut. William Calley Jr.

and the [massacre of civilians] at My Lai. Later followed the Americal's use of the defoliant Agent Orange after it had been banned by the Defense Department. . . . It was a pastiche of units that from the beginning [as Task Force Oregon] were difficult to meld together . . . and it had some of the worst soldiers in the Army. The Americal fought none of the big TV battles, like Khe Sanh, or the seemingly more glamorous war of the helicopter-equipped Airmobile units. Rather, it slugged it out day by day, village by village, in one of the largest, most hostile areas of Vietnam.

Only a few months later, in the *Washington Post* of May 8, 1972, a reporter wrote that "Today most of Chu Lai was empty. The old Americal barracks were falling to rack and ruin. No U.S. fighter-bombers took off from the 10,000-foot runway, now used only by an occasional supply plane. Gone . . . are the scores of helicopters and gunships."

By the end of April 1975, newspapers were covering the swift fall of South Vietnam to victorious VC and NVA troops. "The South Vietnamese capitals that fell were Quang Ngai and Tam Ky. Chu Lai was overrun from Highway 1," a cryptic Associated Press bulletin said.

In May 1985, I received an unexpected call at the office from Mike Pojeski, my old friend from the combat center who was shipped home for mental problems. He was living in California (where else?) and had flown to Montreal to visit Nguyen Ngoc Anh, an interpreter who eventually settled in Canada after the Communist offensive. Somehow Pojeski had found me in Annapolis, and he put Anh on the phone to tell me what he saw during a recent trip back to Vietnam. "*Trung Uy* [Lieutenant] Smith," he said over the crackling phone lines from Montreal, "they would not let me go to Chu Lai, but I saw it as we flew over on the way to Da Nang. There is nothing much left there. I could only see a small patch of airfield remaining."

A month after Pojeski's call, I read in a *Newsweek* magazine article that "The ragged children of Chu Lai comb the sand of the abandoned base . . . which was once the home of the notorious Americal Division . . . , gleaning scrap metal and barbed wire and stuffing it all into old U.S. Army sandbags to drag home."

Finally, in the American Division Association newsletter of January 1991, I read these comments by John M. Wills, a former 198th Brigade soldier who made a sentimental trip back to find what remained of LZ Bayonet:

We stopped a local farmer on the road, and he pointed to where LZ Bayonet was 20 years ago. As I walked through the heavy jungle of what was once the base camp, tears flowed from my eyes. I was able to find the old helo pad where now there is a house in a small clearing . . . But except for what looked like a little asphalt on the ground, LZ Bayonet was gone. It was like it was never there. The only area that isn't overgrown is where the old mess hall was, but I could find no trace that we were ever there. Everything is gone.

On the afternoon I flew away from Chu Lai in late April 1969, of course, I wasn't thinking very far into the future. My mind was on the exceedingly happy present. Duties, responsibilities, and missions were behind me now. My trying tour was finished, and I was merely another army lieutenant with a ticket home. Just another soldier, but a live one.

The C-130 I was riding in was the flying workhorse of the Vietnam War. It was big, reliable, incredibly noisy, and inside stripped of all but the essentials. Passengers sat in facing rows of webbed canvas seats, bobbing and weaving with the jerky motions of the fuselage. Did I mention *noisy*? This plane was equipped with four of the loudest turboprop engines ever bolted to a pair of wings. If you had something to say to anyone aboard, you had to scream it and hope. As the aircraft lost altitude over blue-green Cam Ranh Bay below and banked toward the landing field, I realized fully that my nightmare was over. "It's over," I mumbled to myself, and immediately remembered the famous Roy Orbison song of broken romance, "It's Over," from my teenage years. Those words had a new meaning for me now, however.

What the fuck, I thought, nobody will be able to hear me over the engine din. Hesitantly at first, then with increasing volume and confidence, I began to belt out my own cracked-voice version of "It's Over." No normal person could ever hit his high notes or recreate Orbison's patented rising wall of sound, but at this moment of enormous relief and release, I opened my mouth wide to the words and sang my throat raw. At the exact second I reached my warbling crescendo, the engine noise died away—the pilot was cutting the engines back for landing. Suddenly my amateur rendition of Roy Orbison was reverberating throughout the silenced plane. Fifty of my fellow passengers—hardened veterans all—stared at me in shock. Fifty macho guys heard me humiliating myself, but it was too late to stop.

Who cares anymore, I thought, and threw my arms wide and finished the song with a gawky flourish of notes. Roy Orbison, at least, would have smiled—and so, to my surprise, did my fellow passengers. They were almost certainly all baby boomers who, like me, remembered the song and the artist with fondness. First they grinned at my embarrassment, but then a few joined in. By the time our plane touched down, the surprised crew was listening to fifty-one Roy Orbisons in wrinkled uniforms, joyously rocking and rolling in the back.

It was over.

At Cam Ranh Bay, which seemed like a plush tropical resort compared to Chu Lai and poor little LZ Bayonet, I gorged myself on PX hamburgers and stood under a hot shower for two and a half hours. Early the next morning, I was on an army-chartered airliner, headed east over the South China Sea for home. As we swept over the coast, a lot of the soldiers aboard craned their necks to catch a final glimpse of Vietnam out the windows, but I stared fixedly ahead. I didn't want to give Vietnam even the courtesy of a last look. The twenty-two-hour flight back across the international date line to Fort Lewis, Washington, went quickly, and after a perfect, three-point landing (for which the pilot received a wildly enthusiastic ovation), I stepped off the ramp onto the soil of the United States of America. It hardly needs mentioning that I dropped to my knees and planted a passionate kiss on the ground. Even the runway grease on my lips tasted great.

There was one final problem, however, one more obstacle to overcome.

Fort Lewis was a Stateside military post, one whose activities were apparently run on a peacetime schedule. Returning Vietnam veterans, who were accustomed to twenty-four hour days and seven-day weeks in a combat zone, were in for a shock.

"You'll have to come back Monday morning, gentlemen," the overweight sergeant behind the counter told us. "We're closing up for the weekend."

I was standing at the entrance to the army out-processing center at Fort Lewis at approximately 5:00 P.M. on a cloudy Friday afternoon, only a few hours after I had kissed the good ground of home. While the group of soldiers from our plane had been shuttled through customs, I had become friendly with a Green Beret lieutenant who, like me, was due to be released from active duty as soon as he returned from Vietnam. He had told me he was going to be a music teacher in New England. We had walked over to the out-processing center together, expecting to rush through some paperwork and be officially out of the army within an hour or two—but now this duty sergeant was telling us we would have to wait three more days for freedom.

"C'mon, Sarge, give us a fucking break," my new friend said. "Just stay open long enough to let us process through. We've got people waiting at home for us. Don't make us wait, please?"

"Sorry, sir. It's quitting time. Come back at 0800 on Monday."

"I'm sorry, too, Sergeant," the Green Beret said, removing a .45 automatic from his flight bag and pointing it at the sergeant's chest. "You're just gonna have to postpone your weekend fun a little longer."

When I remember that moment today, I am still surprised that I wasn't particularly shocked at the time. True, the Green Beret had pulled a gun (which the slipshod customs inspection had obviously missed) on the sergeant to force him to let us process out of the army, but on that long-ago afternoon it didn't seem like such a big deal. The Green Beret and I were used to solving problems with guns, after all. We had been in a combat zone, hadn't we?

To the sergeant's credit, he didn't overreact. Perhaps he was used to dealing with crazed Vietnam returnees by that point. In any case, he said "Okay, Lieutenant, you put that pistol away, and you and your buddy can go through." He then called out to his clerks, who were already closing file drawers and putting on their hats, to return to their desks and start our paperwork.

"Go down the line, Eric," the Green Beret said, "and make sure nobody leaves." I did as he asked, thinking that the whole scene reminded me of nothing so much as a bank robbery. But the sergeant was as good as his word, and the Green Beret and I were processed, paid off, and released from the U.S. Army in a little over an hour. We were free to take a taxi to the Seattle-Tacoma airport and fly home to our respective lives.

And that's just what we did, after a vexing overnight wait for plane connections.

Late the next morning, I was belted into my seat on a plane making its final approach to the Knoxville airport, where my wife would be waiting. Because I had heard so many horror stories about hijackers, I kept my right hand inside my flight bag where my own loaded .38 pistol lay in readiness. I was perfectly prepared to blow away any suspicious character I saw heading for the cockpit door. In those days there was little or no airport security, and my weapon hadn't been detected. The stewardess, who had obviously seen many returning Vietnam soldiers before, came up to me and asked gently if I wanted to be seated at the rear of the plane so I could exit before the civilian passengers. "I guess you've got someone you can't wait to see," she said with a smile. I suspect she also wanted to keep a closer watch on what I was so intensely guarding in my flight bag.

"Yes, thank you," I said. It suddenly dawned on me that I really wasn't in a combat zone anymore. I could take my clutched hand off the pistol grip in my bag and relax. No one wanted to kill me now, only help me. I sat there in my monsoon-mildewed khaki uniform with its short row of service ribbons and thanked God for the absence of enemies, for being alive. I took my seat at the back, next to the stewardess.

For nearly a year, I had entertained myself with thoughts of this precious moment. My wife would be standing, I guessed, about fifty yards across the tarmac from the exit ramp of the plane, and I would run to her and pick her up and twirl her around. In dreams I had practiced my every movement—I would dramatically cast my flight bag aside, pull off my overseas cap, and sprint to her waiting arms. Over and over, I had reenacted that ecstatic sequence in my head.

Only it didn't work out that way. It never does.

I stepped into the sunshine outside the plane's door, blinking and looking around for JanElaine.

Damn! She was standing only a few feet from the bottom of the ramp. There would be no chance for that joyous sprint now. I would have to improvise, which is what I had been doing for a year, anyway.

I hurled my flight bag off the ramp, almost beaning a baggage attendant below. Leaping down the ramp steps three at a time, I yanked off my cap and discarded it just barely in time to hit the tarmac and plow awkwardly into JanElaine at full speed, knocking the breath out of both of us.

We laughed and wrapped arms around each other, and kept on laughing all the way home.

It was really over.

# LESSONS

I am, of course, neither a strategist nor a think-tank graduate who can offer high-minded solutions to the military intelligence problems we experienced in Vietnam. I was a junior officer working at a low-level job, both in the field and in base camps located far from the centers of influence. I saw everything at eye level, not from an ivory tower.

Nevertheless, my experience and common sense tell me that there were certain things we could have done to improve the quality of intelligence from enemy prisoners and captured documents. Here, then, are some suggestions that, although they are related to the Vietnam War, could apply to any U.S. military conflict, be it the Persian Gulf War or some future overseas entanglement.

**1.** Make sure you locate the IPW section and the POW cage close to the OB shop—within walking distance, if possible. Interrogators can't talk effectively to detainees without accurate background information, and the OB shop (or whatever it will be called when a new war starts) is the source of that information. If the OB shop is hard to reach, interrogators will be tempted to avoid the hardship and go into an interrogation cold. Any library should be accessible to students and readers, and any OB shop should be accessible to its primary users, the interrogators.

**2.** Use only your best language students, say the top 40 percent, for interrogations, and train enlisted men in the

212

enemy's language as well as you train officers. In Vietnam, we had to rely too much on the quality, loyalty, and availability of our interpreters—an iffy proposition in any foreign conflict. That uncertain reliance can be reduced by assigning the most linguistically skillful officers and enlisted men to IPW duties.

Also, it's a good idea to train your top linguists in interrogation techniques as well. Speaking articulately to a detainee isn't the same as questioning him professionally, as I found out the hard way. I sure wish I had completed that correspondence course in interrogations.

**3.** Make an effort to let capturing units know what happened to the prisoners they turned in and what they said under interrogation. It will motivate the units to capture rather than kill surrendering enemy soldiers, and it may even encourage humane treatment of them on the grounds that uninjured detainees usually give better information. IPW personnel, too, will be happy to see their work helping units in the field. Interrogation reports become classified documents, of course, but a summary system could be devised to tell capturing units the gist of what their prisoners said without disclosing confidential information.

There should also be a direct line of communication between capturing units and IPW sections in the event that information of immediate tactical value is given by a prisoner. Old facts are often useless facts on a fast-moving battlefield, and IPW section leaders ought to have the ability to communicate quickly with commanders in the field.

**4.** U.S. intelligence units and the intelligence units of friendly foreign powers (in Vietnam it was the ARVN) should be in exceedingly close contact, if not in each other's passionate embrace. Too much data fell between the linguistic and operational cracks separating the ARVN and American intelligence communities.

And while we're on this point, I believe that in the future, all foreign interpreters assigned to U.S. units should be under the complete control of U.S. commanders. A lot of problems, disciplinary and otherwise, could have been avoided in Vietnam if the ARVN interpreters had been required to answer to me rather than to their own lax superiors in the ARVN.

5. Now that computers are an integral part of modern warfare, they should be employed as often as feasible in the exploitation of enemy information sources—especially captured documents. The computer data banks I saw at CDEC in Saigon in 1968 could have improved my document analyses substantially if they had been available to me through satellite hookups or other electronic links. Today, more than two decades later, the efficiency of such a system will have increased dramatically—and it ought to be put to use as far down the army intelligence chain of command as possible.